DATE DUE

DE 31 00			
NO 21 01			

DEMCO 38-296

The Japanese Question

The Japanese Question

Power and Purpose in a New Era

Kenneth B. Pyle

The AEI Press

Publisher for the American Enterprise Institute
WASHINGTON, D.C.

1992

Library of Congress Cataloging-in-Publication Data

Pyle, Kenneth B.
    The Japanese question : power and purpose in a new era / Kenneth
B. Pyle.
        p.   cm.
    Includes bibliographical references.
    ISBN 0-8447-3798-4
    1. Japan—Politics and government—1945– 2. World politics—1945–
I. Title. II. Series.
DS889.P95   1992
952.04—dc20   92-756
                                                                        CIP

    3   5   7   9   10   8   6   4   2

The AEI Press
Publisher for the American Enterprise Institute
1150 17th Street, N.W., Washington, D.C. 20036

Printed in the United States of America

For Anne

Contents

Acknowledgments

This book is an outcome of a multiyear project on "Economic Interdependence and Defense Burden-Sharing in the Pacific Basin" undertaken jointly by the American Enterprise Institute and the Henry M. Jackson School of International Studies at the University of Washington. The project was funded by the Pew Charitable Trust as part of its research program on integrating economics and national security. I am grateful to the Pew Trust for its support as well as to the John M. Olin Foundation for sabbatical leave support during 1988–1989, when parts of this book were written.

Portions of this book appeared in different forms in essays I wrote for other books and journals. I want to express appreciation to the Society for Japanese Studies for permission to include material originally presented in my articles "The Future of Japanese Nationality, An Essay in Contemporary History," *Journal of Japanese Studies*, vol. 8, no. 2 (Summer 1982), pp. 223–64; "In Pursuit of a Grand Design: Nakasone betwixt the Past and Future," *Journal of Japanese Studies*, vol. 13, no. 2 (Summer 1987), pp. 243–70; and "Japan's New Internationalism: Struggling with the Burdens of History," in Kozo Yamamura, ed., *Japanese Investment in the United States: Should We Be Concerned?* (Seattle: Society for Japanese Studies, 1989). I also want to express appreciation to Stanford University Press for permission to include material from my chapter "Japan, the World, and the Twenty-first Century," in Takashi Inoguchi and Daniel I. Okimoto, eds., *The Political Economy of Japan*, vol. 2, *The Changing International Context* (Stanford: Stanford University Press, 1988). Portions of chapters 4 and 6 of this present book appear in Henry Bienen, ed., *Power, Economic Relations, and Security: An Overview with U.S.-Japan Cases* (Boulder:

Westview Press, 1992), which is also a product of the Pew Charitable Trust research program on integrating economics and national security. I also want to acknowledge the support of the United States Institute of Peace: the last chapter of the present book is based on a paper presented in the spring of 1991 to a USIP-sponsored conference.

Finally, I want to express my deepest sense of obligation and gratitude to my parents and my parents-in-law and above all to my wife, Anne, for so many things that I cannot here begin to name them.

The Japanese Question

1

Introduction

Only rarely in modern history has a nation captured so substantial a fraction of international trade in such a short period as Japan has in the past three decades. Previous instances of such a rapid increase of relative economic power provoked strong reaction in other countries. Japan's rise has provoked a particularly negative reaction because of its history of imperial expansionism. The Japanese resurgence has raised questions as to what purpose this power will be put in the future and what role Japan will play in the international system. These questions assume even greater importance because of the flux in the international system brought about by the end of the cold war.

This book is a study of Japan's formulation of its national purpose in the post–World War II period. Throughout this period Japan single-mindedly pursued its own commercial interests, avoiding involvement in international political-strategic affairs and shunning controversial issues in its foreign relations. Its behavior often seemed more appropriate to an international trading firm than to a nation-state. Foreign observers ordinarily understood Japan's political passivity as the result of popular pacifism and the restraints of an imposed constitutional order. To an extent this understanding is accurate. These factors clearly established parameters within which postwar Japanese political leadership had to operate.

Much more than has been commonly recognized, however, Japan's purpose in the postwar period was the result of the conservative leaders' opportunistic adaptation to the circumstances of the international order. The cold war structure of international politics allowed Japan to rely on the United States to

3

guarantee its security and at the same time to maintain the international free trade order, while Japan was free to follow policies of economic nationalism. Prime Minister Yoshida Shigeru and his successors not only formulated an economics-first policy and depended on the U.S. security guarantee; they also chose to interpret the constitution so narrowly as to frustrate all attempts to engage Japan in collective security commitments. This strategy was a brilliant success. In contrast to every other major power, Japan was spared the domestic controversy and disruption that an active foreign policy would have engendered and was free to concentrate its resources and energies on achieving economic growth.

Benefiting from uniquely favorable political-economic circumstances, the nation achieved its century-old goal of overtaking the industrial powers of the West. Partly as a result of the sharply negative reaction abroad to its mercantilist policies and partly because the nation's position in the world had dramatically shifted, this achievement stimulated a reassessment of Japanese purpose at the outset of the 1980s. A neoconservative agenda formulated during the administrations of Prime Ministers Ōhira Masayoshi and Nakasone Yasuhiro proposed a new and broader sense of the national interest. Acknowledging that Japan could no longer act as a follower in the international system, this agenda included a program of institutional reform that would open Japan to international influences and an activist foreign policy intended to convert Japan to international leadership.

Accomplishing such a historic shift of national purpose proved exceedingly difficult. The institutional legacy of its long struggle to overtake the West hobbled the systemic transformation that was envisioned by the neoconservatives. Change came about only as a reaction to external events rather than as a response to this newly articulated national purpose. Because of the powerful momentum created by its modern history, the principal motive forces of national life continued to be the economic dynamism of Japanese firms, the existing political-economic framework within which they operated, and the values of economic rationality that drove them.

At the beginning of the 1990s, the grudging and limited Japanese contribution to the international coalition in the Persian Gulf raised anew the question of Japan's future national purpose, its policies toward collective security arrangements, and its capacity to change from a country intent on its own economic aims to one capable of becoming an international leader. In one area, however, the emergence of a prominent Japanese international role seems inescapable. The powerful economic forces dominating its national life are propelling Japan toward leadership in the Pacific basin. What form this leadership will take is an open question. Much depends on U.S. initiatives in the post–cold war era to fashion new institutions, including a revised U.S.-Japan alliance, to fit the changed circumstances of the region.

2

The Question of a
Resurgent Japan

In an era of headlong change, while Europe is struggling with the German question in determining its new order, Asia has the Japanese question to confront as a fundamental issue in charting the future. Both questions arise from a widespread belief that twentieth-century history reveals traits of national character that require special precautions and arrangements. The specter of a resurgent Japan, a Japan of great economic power and uncertain national purpose, troubles Asia and the Japanese-American alliance. While Asians talk openly about the Japanese question, Americans, because of their alliance with Japan, tended to avoid the issues after 1948, when the occupation ceased to reform Japan and began to rehabilitate the nation as its leading cold war ally in Asia. The Japanese question, however, should be addressed because it is fundamental to the resolution of the paradoxes and anomalies in the present Japanese-American relationship. With the end of the cold war, these paradoxes and anomalies can no longer be overlooked.

One can imagine that some future student of history looking back at the early 1990s might wonder why the world's largest debtor nation continued to provide the security for the world's largest creditor nation. How was it that the United States continued by treaty to provide a unilateral security guarantee for the Japanese state while it was running more than a $40 billion annual trade deficit with that state? How was it that the United States continued to commit more than 45,000 military personnel to the defense of Japan while a majority of Americans regarded Japan's economic power as a greater threat than the power of any other country's?

Part of the answer to these questions is that the United States gave primacy to the demands of the cold war and thus decided grudgingly to live with these peculiarities and paradoxes of the U.S.-Japan alliance. Part of the answer relates to the extraordinary foreign policy of postwar Japan, which chose to concentrate exclusively on economic growth, to remain lightly armed, and to trade bases on Japanese soil in return for an American security guarantee.

Part of the answer, too, lies in a fundamental, often unspoken, question in the minds of U.S. policy makers: can Japan be trusted to participate responsibly in international security affairs? This Japanese question is at the core of American thinking about its alliance with Japan and beclouds the issue of how Japan should contribute to the maintenance of the international order upon which it depends so heavily for its remarkable affluence. As the cold war comes to an end in Asia as it has in Europe, this concern must be resolved, for it is fundamental to the continued relationship of the United States and Japan and to the potential role of Japan in the changing pattern of international relations in East Asia.[1]

Mindful of Japanese nationalism and militarism, world leaders are intensely ambivalent as to whether Japan should enlarge its security role. Prompted by a fear of revived Japanese nationalism, U.S. leaders are extremely circumspect toward Japan. This feeling recurs throughout Asia, in the Soviet Union, and in Europe—indeed in Japan itself. Soon after he left the prime ministership in 1987, Nakasone Yasuhiro brooded about such persistent international distrust of Japan:

> Other countries, especially those against whom we committed aggression and our neighboring countries whom we victimized, see little difference between Germany and Japan. I think a century must pass before the suspicion and distrust of our neighbors will dissipate. Of course Hitler's philosophy and methods were fundamentally different from those of Japan. . . . Moreover, not only is Japan economically and technologically powerful, as a people (*minzoku*) we have strong solidarity, our labor and management cooperate, and we have a remarkable sense of public order. In these circumstances, and because we are a population of 120 million, neighboring states inevitably fear us.[1]

The Occupation and the Japanese Question

Japan's empire building in the 1930s and 1940s created a seemingly indelible image of a national character with an irrational and fanatical dimension. Belief in the historically rooted militarism of the Japanese was one of General Douglas MacArthur's motivations for inserting Article 9 in the postwar Japanese constitution. "For centuries," he said, "the Japanese people, unlike their neighbors in the Pacific Basin—the Chinese, the Malayans, the Indians, and the Whites—have been students and idolaters of the art of war and the warrior caste."[2]

American idealism was at high tide when MacArthur in February 1946 ordered his staff to draft a model constitution to serve as a guide for the Japanese. The U.S. intention was to ensure that the sources of Japanese militarism were rooted out through fundamental reforms of Japanese government, society, and economic structure. In every aspect, Japan should be democratized, for MacArthur was convinced that a democracy would never make war. MacArthur, however, believed that militarism was historically ingrained in the Japanese experience, and he therefore instructed his subordinates to insert a clause in the constitution renouncing war and armament. The precise origin of this idea will likely never be known. MacArthur insisted that Prime Minister Shidehara Kijūrō broached the idea to him. If this is so, Shidehara most likely was responding to cues from occupation officials. At the time the concept surfaced, the fate of the emperor was still undetermined, and Japanese leaders were at great pains to do whatever was necessary to prevent the trial of the emperor as a war criminal and the abolition of the imperial institution. Japanese leaders consequently accepted the constitution, including Article 9, as the price they had to pay to preserve the institution, albeit in the form of a constitutional monarchy.

The notion of renouncing war as an instrument of national policy was not uncommon in the post–World War I years. In 1928 the leading nations of the world (including Japan) concluded the General Treaty for the Renunciation of War, better known as the Kellogg-Briand Pact, which condemned "recourse to war as a solution of international controversies." The idea of placing some such provision in a constitution gained popularity in the 1930s when Congressman Louis Ludlow proposed an amendment to the U.S. Constitution providing that except in case of attack on U.S. territory or on any other country in the Western hemisphere, "the people shall have the sole power by a national referendum to declare war or to engage in warfare overseas."[3] Perhaps most interesting of all, the 1935 constitution of the Philippines, approved by President Franklin Roosevelt, contained a provision stating that "the Philippines renounces war as an instrument of national policy."[4]

Nevertheless, despite the currency of renouncing war as an instrument of policy, the notion of a unilateral disarmament was not generally intended in these examples. Signatories to the Kellogg-Briand Pact declared that its provisions did not preclude self-defense or collective security arrangements. Similarly it is doubtful that many U.S. policy makers intended to deprive Japan of the power of self-defense. In fact, in the autumn of 1945 MacArthur received instructions from Washington and an indication that the new political order in Japan should establish the supremacy of civilian control over the military—clearly implying the continuation of a Japanese military force. Nonetheless, renunciation of war as an instrument of national policy—the Kellogg-Briand concept—was on many people's minds in the war-weary days after the Japanese surrender. The emperor himself used this phrase in a statement to foreign newsmen in September 1945. Moreover, in his January 1, 1946, rescript denying his own divinity, he spoke of constructing a new Japan "through thoroughly being pacific." The emperor's advisers were anxious to preserve the imperial institution by demonstrating his commitment to the establishment of a peaceful order.

MacArthur, captivated by the high idealism of the early occupation and expecting that collective security arrangements through the United Nations were being put in place, seemed prepared to leave Japan wholly disarmed. He therefore instructed his aide, General Courtney Whitney, that in the new Japanese constitution "war as a sovereign right of the nation is abolished. Japan renounces it as an instrumentality for settling its disputes and even for preserving its own security." Nevertheless, when Colonel Charles Kades, who was the principal drafter of the model constitution that the occupation presented to the Japanese cabinet, left out the phrase "even for preserving its own security" because he said it was "unrealistic" for a nation to lack the right of self-defense, both Whitney and MacArthur acquiesced.[5]

Moreover, when the draft constitution was considered by the Diet, Ashida Hitoshi, chairman of the lower house committee reviewing the draft, made two significant amendments. He inserted two phrases with far-reaching implications. One, preceding the first sentence of Article 9, reads: "Aspiring sincerely to an international peace based on justice and order." The other, preceding the second sentence of that article, reads: "For the above purpose." The upper house subsequently changed this phrase to read, "In order to accomplish the aim of the preceding paragraph" so that Article 9 as finally adopted reads:

> Aspiring sincerely to an international peace based on justice and order, the Japanese people forever renounce war as a sovereign right of the nation and the threat or use of force as a means of settling international disputes.
>
> In order to accomplish the aim of the preceding paragraph, land, sea, and air forces, as well as other war potential, will never be maintained. The right of belligerency of the state will not be recognized.

Kades approved these amendments with the understanding that they could be interpreted to mean that war and the threat or use of force were renounced only as a means of settling international disputes. War and a resort to force were not forbidden in matters of self-defense. Kades therefore understood the amendments to enable Japan to maintain self-defense forces as well as to permit the contribution of an armed contingent to a United Nations international force. These points are worth emphasizing since they bear on Japan's potential role in collective security arrangements. A number of cabinet members, including Shidehara and Yoshida Shigeru, were concerned that Article 9 might prevent Japan from ever joining the United Nations because of the provision in the UN Charter obligating its members to make available to the Security Council "armed forces . . . for the purpose of maintaining international peace and security." Kades concluded that the occupation had no intention of denying the right to self-defense or participation in UN peace-keeping forces.[6]

Ashida, who later served as prime minister for a brief period in 1948, asserted after the occupation was ended that his amendments were intended to make defensive wars and self-defense forces permissible and constitutional. Apparently, few Diet members at the time grasped this point during the review of the draft constitution. The Far Eastern Commission, the Allied body established to advise the occupation, however, realized the possibility of rearmament as a result of the Ashida amendments. The Chinese delegate to the FEC angrily accused the Japanese of planning "to deceive the world into thinking that Japan was absolutely renouncing military forces when actually they planned to rearm the country using the loopholes created by the textual changes in the constitution."[7] Accordingly, the FEC insisted on the insertion of a provision in the constitution that all ministers of state be civilian as a way of ensuring civilian control of the military. Article 66, which states that "the Prime Minister and other Ministers of State must be civilians," thus clearly implies permission to possess military power.

In sum, while determined to root out the sources of militarism in Japan and to democratize the social order, the drafters did not intend that the new constitutional order should deprive Japan of the capacity for self-defense or normal participation in the newly contemplated UN peace-keeping forces. On the contrary, the contention that the constitution constrained the establishment of self-defense forces or participation in the United Nations and other multilateral security arrangements was devised by Japanese politicians for subsequent political purpose. This constitutional interpretation, as shown in chapter 3, became a convenient pretext for a national purpose that was subsequently formulated by Prime Minister Yoshida to avoid all collective security involvements, to abstain from international politics, to avoid intense domestic political conflict, and to concentrate exclusively on economic rehabilitation.

Subsequent Views of the Japanese Question

When the occupation gave way to an alliance in the cold war, concern over Japanese trustworthiness was largely repressed, although it was always present below the surface. To some observers, Japan's postwar single-minded pursuit of economic growth itself seemed virtual proof of an extremist trait in the national character. Urging Japan to rearm worried former secretary of defense Harold Brown because "the Japanese, as their economic activities show, do not do things by halves."[8] The leaders of other countries were more blunt. Edith Cresson, who became French prime minister in 1991, had remarked a year earlier that "Japan has an absolute will to conquer the world" and urged her government to put together a "combat strategy" to fight for market shares in data processing, electronics, high-definition television, and other fields. In the light of such sentiments in the West and Japan's growing domination of the Asian economy, the president of South Korea's Hyundai corporation asked, "Does Japan intend to fight the world?"[9]

George Ball, former under secretary of state, elaborated on this view of Japanese character. Rearming Japan was dangerous, he argued, because "you never know when the Japanese will go ape." Following the enunciation of the Nixon (Guam) Doctrine and in the aftermath of the 1971 Nixon shocks, he cautioned the Nixon administration against its rough treatment of Japan, describing the Japanese as a people motivated by "pride, nationalism, and often downright irrationality." Ball saw a historical pattern of sudden, careening changes of Japanese national course:

> Japanese history has never been charted by the same kind of wavering curve that has marked the progress of other countries; instead it resembles more a succession of straight lines, broken periodically by sharp angles as the whole nation, moving full speed, has suddenly wheeled like a well-drilled army corps to follow a new course. There is nothing in all human experience to match it.

Those sharp angles moved the nation from a closed country to unreserved borrowing from the West in the nineteenth century, from all-out imperialism to persistent commercial pursuit since World War II. This character trait implied something dangerous and unpredictable in the Japanese people.[10]

A strong generational experience influences U.S. concern about Japanese nationalism. President George Bush was shot down in the Pacific by the Japanese. Many leading members of the Reagan administration, such as Secretary of State George Shultz and Secretary of Defense Caspar Weinberger, saw service against Japan. Reagan's secretary of commerce, the late Malcolm Baldrige, fought on Iwo Jima when he was a twenty-two-year-old infantry lieutenant. He spoke movingly of the memories of hand-to-hand combat with Japanese guerrillas. Of the 180 men in Baldrige's company who landed on Okinawa, only 20 survived. As a matter of policy, he was reluctant to link trade with security issues and to press Japan for substantially greater security contributions in return for U.S. trade concessions.

In 1985 an esteemed American journalist evoked Japanese militarism in a harsh anti-Japanese essay in the *New York Times*. Theodore White likened the 1930s drive for empire with the 1980s drive for markets: "Today the Japanese are on the move again in one of history's most brilliant commercial offensives, as they go about dismantling American industry."[11]

A British correspondent stationed in Hong Kong warned of a revival in Japan of Yamatoism, an "irrational national mysticism" that he tied to Japanese trade strategy: "The conflict with Japan today is economic not military. And Yamatoism is an emotional defense when foreigners attack Japan's adversarial trade tactics." Ian Buruma, writing in the *New York Times Magazine* called Japan's political economy a "state capitalism bolstered by blood and soil mythology." In his view the Japanese political economy combined with an ultranationalist ideology to produce a nation incited by destructive and irrational forces.[12]

Few events in postwar Japan so provoked concern over the Japanese question as the bizarre suicide on November 25, 1970, of Mishima Yukio, the novelist who had been nominated for the Nobel Prize. Reflecting on the event, Henry Scott Stokes, editor of *Harper's*, longtime journalist in Japan with the *New York Times* and the *Times* of London, and friend and biographer of Mishima, wrote that the remilitarization of Japan was "a deeply unsettling prospect" because of "the hallowed tradition of self-destruction which is at the heart of Japanese culture and history," a tradition epitomized by Mishima's suicide. Scott Stokes believed that Mishima's act struck a responsive chord among Japanese who were "deeply traumatized" by the constitution that was forced upon them and that required the abandonment of ancient traditions of martial valor, replaced by materialist and merchant values. Mishima, who had organized a small army of rightist students, was privately helped by Satō Eisaku, the prime minister, and Nakasone, who was director-general of the Japan Defense Agency at the time. Satō's connections with right-wing businessmen facilitated financial support for Mishima's small militia, and Nakasone made it possible for it to train at a Self-Defense Forces base. Satō, Nakasone, and many other prominent Japanese sympathized with Mishima's effort to revive the "withered soul" of Japan. "Mishima was not so much an aberrant Japanese as an extreme but exemplary metaphor for Japan's frustrations with its dependent foreign policy."[13]

Mishima's appeal was to the dark and tragic side of his country. Ivan Morris, one of the leading interpreters of Japanese civilization and a friend of Mishima, traced this aspect of national character in his *Nobility of Failure*. In contrast to the more familiar achievement-oriented Japanese, the good company man whose hard work, dedication, and discipline typify Japanese character in recent times, the complex Japanese culture also has a tradition of the tragic hero who refuses to compromise sincerity and principle for the realism required for success in the world.

As Japan's economic power mounted during the 1980s, the Japanese question came to focus not only on the dark aspects of

13

past actions but on the uncertainties of Japan's future intentions. To what purpose was this immense new power to be put? James Fallows, Washington editor of *Atlantic Monthly*, in a phrase evoking the origins of U.S. cold war strategy, advocated "containing Japan." Fallows argued that Japan was unable or unwilling to "restrain the one-sided and destructive expansion of its economic power." Weak in universal principles, the Japanese did not easily identify with other peoples, and it was "hard to imagine that Mitsubishi, Matsushita, the Dai-Ichi Kangyo Bank, or any of Japan's other great power centers will ever share their power with non-Japanese."[14] Similarly, R. Taggart Murphy, an American banker in Tokyo, observed that "the only real ideology Japan has is an overwhelming sense of its own uniqueness." Sitting on "the largest cache of wealth ever assembled," Japan possessed "power without purpose" and was unfit to exercise responsible international leadership: "Lacking the ideology, Japan will not sacrifice its own interests for the interests of the global financial system."[15] Japan's adversarial trade practices were increasingly seen as undermining the international free trade order. An American specialist on the Japanese economy, Leon Hollerman, argued that Japan was pursuing a strategy to make itself a "headquarters nation" in the world economy. Japan's business and political elites were collaborating in institutional arrangements designed to achieve economic security and reduced vulnerability by ensuring "stability in its foreign markets and sources of supply; suppression of financial, technological, and political risk; and a position of acknowledged leadership in both a regional and a global context."[16]

In 1990, in the midst of a spate of such writings that reflected international skepticism about Japanese intentions, a translation of a chauvinist tract by two prominent Japanese provoked further apprehension about Japanese purpose. Clearly not intended for foreign readership, *The Japan That Can Say No* by Ishihara Shintarō and Morita Akio exhorted the Japanese to confront foreign demands regarding their trade practices with a defiant no that would demonstrate Japan's new independence and assertiveness. Ishihara, a popular novelist turned flamboyant politician who had been repeatedly elected to the Diet, had twice held cabinet posts, and had been a candidate for prime minister, gloated over Japanese economic strength and proposed using Japan's technological prowess as a means of bringing the United States to heel. Morita, chairman of the Sony Corporation, expressed similar views in more measured tones, but the fact that so prominent a leader of

Japanese business chose to join with an outspoken nationalist in producing this strident tract could only amplify mistrust of the purposes to which Japanese economic power would be put. It left the impression of the Japanese as unpredictable in their future international role.[17]

The Japanese themselves often seem as distrustful of their national character as foreign observers. To take one example, the prominent anthropologist Nakane Chie, recognized for her work on the structure of Japanese society and for her theory of an unchanging Japanese character, summarized her fears:

> The Japanese way of thinking depends on the situation rather than principle—while with the Chinese it is the other way around. . . . We Japanese have no principles. Some people think we hide our intentions, but we have no intentions to hide. Except for a few leftists or rightists, we have no dogma and don't ourselves know where we are going. This is a risky situation, for if someone is able to mobilize this population in a certain direction, we have no checking mechanism. . . . If we establish any goal we will proceed to attain it without considering any other factors. It is better for us to remain just as we are. For if we are set in motion toward any direction, we have just too much energy and no mechanism to check its direction.[18]

Such fears about their own national character are expressed not only by people outside of the government but by members of the ruling party itself. At the time of the Persian Gulf Crisis in 1990, when Japanese leaders were debating legislation to permit dispatch of the Self-Defense Forces to participate in the international coalition, Gotōda Masaharu, a senior member of the Liberal Democratic party, expressed opposition to any change in the constitution because then "all restraints would disappear. A great economic power would become a great military power."[19] Gotōda, a respected conservative politician who had served as director of the National Police Agency and as chief cabinet secretary in the Nakasone administration (1982–1987), helped defeat a government plan in 1987, during the Iran-Iraq conflict, to send SDF minesweepers to the gulf because he believed it essential to maintain legal restraints on Japanese rearmament. As the economist Nakatani Iwao observed, one would expect Socialist and Communist party leaders to express this kind of reason for maintaining restraints, but for an LDP leader to see them necessary to prevent Japan from "going wild" (bōsō suru) was "deeply wounding" to the nation's self-image.[20]

The pressure that the U.S. government applied on Japan to make a token contribution of personnel to the coalition forces in the Persian Gulf likewise excited alarm in some quarters in the United States, where it was feared that it would encourage a revival of militarism. A veteran columnist and former East Asian correspondent of the *New York Times*, A. M. Rosenthal, saw it as an ominous turning point:

> The United States is working hard, doing its very best, to persuade Japan to make a momentous decision. If Japan finally agrees, generations to come will remember and study the great historic moment—and will curse the day. . . .
>
> Count on this: The Japanese Army will soon again become a political force at home, a constant threat to the delicate, complex civilian equilibrium that is now the base and protection of Japan's democratic society.[21]

A more reasoned explanation was offered by a Dutch journalist, Karel van Wolferen, whose recent book analyzing the Japanese political system emphasized the weakness and diffusion of Japanese executive power. He suggested that an expanded military "would be a potentially uncontrollable force. . . . As frustrated economic negotiators have discovered in the past decade, no one is in charge of the Japanese state as a whole. The powerful bureaucracies do not answer to voters. There is no center of political accountability."[22]

As cold war tensions disappear, the Japanese question is certain to surface more often in discussions of the future purpose of the Japanese-American alliance. As a recent example, Fred Hiatt, a *Washington Post* correspondent, reported on March 27, 1990, that the top Marine Corps general in Japan, Major General Henry C. Stackpole III, said that U.S. troops must remain in Japan at least until the beginning of the twenty-first century in large part because "no one wants a rearmed, resurgent Japan. So we are a cap in the bottle, if you will." As the general elaborated, the concern over Japanese fanaticism was once again clear: "The Japanese consider themselves racially superior. They feel they have a handle on the truth and their economic growth has proved that. They have achieved the Greater Asia Co-Prosperity Sphere economically, without guns." The general was publicly rebuked by an assistant secretary of defense, Henry Rowen, for suggesting that the Mutual Security Treaty was predicated on distrust of Japan, but the general's remarks underscored the persistence of the Japanese question as a central concern of U.S. policy makers.

Another factor keeping the Japanese question alive is the widespread impression internationally that Japan's conservative leadership has never dealt forthrightly with the issue of World War II. While many Japanese have been severely self-critical in assessing Japan's responsibility, mainstream conservative political leaders have not. For them the war revealed no fundamental flaw of national character, nor even a fault in the prewar emperor system. It was rather an aberration—postwar Prime Minister Yoshida Shigeru dismissed it as a "historic stumble"—an interlude in which military conspiracy, left-wing planning, and diplomatic blunders deflected the Japanese from their legitimate goals pursued since the Meiji Restoration. The Great Depression and "the breakdown of a stable world order created the situation in which unrest, conspiracy, and plain diplomatic ineptitude" had caused Japan's aberration.[23]

During the 1980s a series of highly publicized incidents confirmed the persistence of this conservative view. In 1986 Prime Minister Nakasone dismissed the education minister, Fujio Masayuki, for arguing that the colonization of Korea had been legitimate and that the rape of Nanking did not violate international law.[24] In May 1988 the director general of the National Land Agency, Okuno Seisuke, had to be dismissed from the cabinet by Prime Minister Takeshita Noboru for public remarks glossing over Japanese responsibility for the invasion of China during the 1930s. Less than a year later, Takeshita himself, on the eve of Emperor Shōwa's funeral, expressed uncertainty about Japanese responsibility for aggression in World War II and was even vague as to whether Hitler's policies constituted aggression.

Such continuing incidents make the formal, carefully scripted apologies that Japanese leaders offer for past aggression seem contrived and insincere. Helmut Schmidt frequently asserts that Germany has been much more successful in coming to terms with its past than Japan. Consequently "we Germans have been lucky enough to find a great number of friends and allies among our immediate neighbors in Europe." Schmidt adds that Japan has only one half-hearted friend, its ally the United States, because the Japanese have not disowned their past sins:

> They have to repent. And that is one of the distinctions between the behavior of the Japanese and my country for instance. I mean, they have been too proud to repent, and I think this has been a great mistake on the side of the Japanese. . . . They need to show the other nations in

17

the area, from Korea down to Singapore, that they de-
plore what has been done in the name of Japan.[25]

Fundamental to the Japanese question is the future course of
Japan's relations with Asia. That is, a key test of Japan's national
purpose, its claims to be forging an internationalist foreign policy
and a capacity for international leadership, will be the way it
exerts its rapidly rising influence in Asia. Many of the issues that
keep alive a deep distrust of Japanese purpose have to do with a
perception that the Japanese still hold their traditional disregard,
insensitivity, and disdain for other Asians.

A veteran Japanese diplomat, Asai Motofumi, who recently
retired from the foreign service and became an adviser to the
Socialist party, wrote in 1989 in a widely noted book on Japanese
foreign policy that true internationalization could only be achieved
when Japan adopted a new attitude toward Asia. "Japan's sense
of superiority toward the rest of Asia," he wrote, "is un-
changed."[26] He described the conservative leadership as unrepen-
tant for the destruction done to Asia in World War II, as demonstrated by their continuing efforts to revise textbook accounts of
Japanese aggression and by their official visits to the Yasukuni
Shrine, which honored the exploits of the Japanese military in
Asia.

Leadership in Asia is an old Japanese ambition. The founders
of the modern state in the mid-nineteenth century commonly
advocated it as a national goal. Even the great liberal educator
Fukuzawa Yukichi exclaimed in an unguarded moment in 1882,
"We are Japanese and we shall someday raise the national power
of Japan so that not only shall we control the natives of China and
India as the English do today, but we shall also possess in our
hands the power to rebuke the English and to rule Asia ourselves."[27]

In the 1930s Japan determined to drive Anglo-American influence from Asia and to establish regional self-sufficiency under
Japanese military domination. The Greater East Asia Co-Prosperity Sphere was to be a vertical order, presided over by the superior
Japanese, with all other Asians finding their "proper place" in the
hierarchy of peoples or races based on inherent qualities and
capabilities. A report produced by Japanese bureaucrats during
World War II demonstrated the racist views that Japanese leaders
held toward other Asians. The goal of the new order was to create
"an economic structure which would ensure the permanent subordination of all other peoples and nations of Asia to Japan." As

the "leading race" of Asia, Japan had a national mission to organize other peoples while preserving its own purity. Although local customs and traditions should be respected so long as they did not conflict with Japanese interests, the supremacy of Japanese culture was unquestioned. Reference to "proper place" in the Co-Prosperity Sphere meant that there should be a division of labor with each people performing economic functions for which their inherent capabilities prepared them. "In this scheme," writes the historian John Dower, who uncovered the government report,

> Japan was the towering metropole, the overwhelmingly dominant hub of the great autarkic bloc. All currency and finance would naturally be tied to the yen. All major transportation and communication networks, whether on land or by sea or air, were to center on Japan and be controlled by Tokyo. All war-related industrial production, energy sources, and strategic materials would likewise be centralized and controlled by Japan, and, in general, Japan would be responsible for the production of high quality manufactures and finished products in the heavy-industry sector. While Japan would provide capital and technical know-how for the development of light industry (generally for local consumption) throughout the Co-Prosperity Sphere, most countries would remain in their familiar roles as producers of raw materials and semifinished goods.[28]

This vertical division of labor, the report argued, would benefit all Asians, but its ultimate goal was to create "an inseparable economic relationship between the Yamato race, the leader of the East Asia Cooperative Body, and other member peoples, whereby our country will hold the key to the very existence of all the races of East Asia."[29]

In the postwar period, Japan's relations with the rest of Asia were distant and largely limited to trade. Conservative leadership, as discussed in chapter 3, resisted all efforts to engage Japan in collective security agreements with other Asian nations. In contrast, West Germany sought entry into NATO as a way of integrating itself with the rest of Europe, of anchoring the Federal Republic to the West, and of diminishing concern over the German question. Germany's motivations were absent in Tokyo. In the 1990s, however, the vast new dimensions of Japanese economic influence in the region portend a much more prominent role in the politics of Asia and a critical testing of Japanese character and purpose.

3

Japan's Postwar National Purpose

Throughout the postwar decades, Japan's role in the world was a product of the political order imposed on it by the victors and the shrewd and pragmatic policies of postwar Japanese leaders. While forging to the front rank of global economic power, Japan remained politically withdrawn, shunning initiatives and involvement in political-strategic issues. This role as a trading nation, aloof from international politics, was supported by a remarkably durable popular consensus.

Japan's passivity in the international politics of the postwar era is ordinarily interpreted as a product of wartime trauma, unconditional surrender, popular pacifism, nuclear allergy, restraints of a peace constitution, and sometimes bureaucratic immobilism. All of these factors are without question ingredients in forming Japan's postwar international role; they established the parameters within which political leadership operated. Nevertheless, we miss the essence of postwar Japanese political history if we overlook evidence that the fundamental orientation toward economic growth and political passivity was also the product of a carefully constructed and brilliantly implemented foreign policy. That is, much more than has been commonly recognized, Japan's purpose in the postwar world was the result of an opportunistic adaptation to the conditions in which the Japanese leadership found their nation and a shrewd pursuit of a sharply defined national interest within the constraints that the postwar international order placed upon them.

The Yoshida Doctrine

The key figure in shaping the postwar conception of Japanese national purpose was Yoshida Shigeru, who was prime minister for seven of the first eight and one-half years of the postwar period and who served concurrently as foreign minister during much of this time. In the desolation and despair of the postwar days, when Japan was a virtual international pariah and the nation's fortunes were at the lowest point in history, Yoshida gradually put together a sense of national purpose that has guided the country to the present.

His conception of national purpose far outlived his own career in part because he gathered around him a group of political disciples known as the Yoshida school, who carried on his influence in the decades after he left office. In particular, two of his proteges, Ikeda Hayato and Satō Eisaku (known as the honor students of the Yoshida school) during their tenures as prime minister in the 1960s and 1970s, elaborated the implications of Yoshida's vision of Japan's fundamental purpose and orientation in the world.[1]

In addition to his success in installing a powerful group of followers in the conservative ruling party and in the bureaucracy to carry on his policies, Yoshida's influence endured because of his extraordinary skill in perceiving world trends and in using them to the advantage of Japan's special needs. He had a clear sense of the strengths and potentialities, as well as the limitations, of the Japanese nation. From these insights he was able to fashion an enduring concept of the national interest as the nature of the postwar international order took shape.

A veteran diplomat and long-time student of diplomatic history, Yoshida had an unusual sense of the possibilities that changes in international politics might offer. At the time that he formed his first cabinet in the spring of 1946, he observed to a colleague that "history provides examples of winning by diplomacy after losing in war (*sensō de makete gaikō de katta rekishi wa aru*)."[2] That is, a defeated nation, by analyzing and exploiting the shifting relations among world powers, could contain the damage incurred in defeat and could instead win the peace. Yoshida knew that disputes between victors over the postwar settlement with the defeated nation could be used to the latter's advantage. The cold war offered just such an opportunity.

In the immediate postwar period, Yoshida's primary concern in foreign affairs was to restore Japan's reputation and to have the nation accepted by the international community. This entailed convincing world opinion that Japan had changed and that the Japanese people were indeed committed to a new, peaceful course. So ostracized was Japan that extreme statements of Japan's utter commitment to change were required to convince world opinion. As a matter of political expediency, therefore, some of the most uncompromising statements of the pacifist ideal unsurprisingly came from Yoshida himself. Before 1950, Yoshida unqualifiedly and consistently expressed his support of Japanese disarmament. As he said in a radio broadcast on the first anniversary of surrender, "The new constitution provides for renunciation of war, in which regard Japan leads the rest of the world. . . . Now that we have been beaten, and we haven't got a single soldier left on our hands, it is a fine opportunity of renouncing war for all time." More than three years later, in November 1949, he addressed the Diet in no less uncompromising terms: "It is my belief that the very absence of armaments is a guarantee of the security and happiness of our people, and *will gain for us the confidence of the world*, and will enable us as a peaceful nation to take pride before the world in our national polity."[3]

Yoshida needed the confidence of the world because he was intent on an early end to the occupation, and he ordered the bureaucracy to undertake a far-reaching inquiry into Japan's strategic options. The study convinced him of what his instincts had already sensed: Japan's long-range interests lay in a bilateral military agreement with the United States, as the new world power, and the United States was unlikely to relinquish its military position in Japan in the near future. If Japan were to gain its independence, that is, an end to the occupation, any time soon, it would be necessary to offer the Americans continued access to bases inside Japan. In the prewar period, Yoshida had been an advocate of a close Anglo-Japanese relation. He now determined that Japan should associate itself with the Americans, the new hegemonic power, as closely as practicable. But this did not entail a sacrifice of the national interest to the U.S. purpose. On the contrary, as he said, perhaps half-seriously, "Just as the United States was once a colony of Great Britain but is now the stronger of the two, if Japan becomes a colony of the United States, it will also eventually become the stronger."[4] Japan could look to its long-range interest by assuming for the time being a subordinate role within the U.S. international order. Therefore, in May 1950 he dispatched his protege, Ikeda Hayato, to Washington to offer bases for an early return of national sovereignty.

Negotiating independence and a bilateral military agreement with the United States compelled Yoshida to formulate in much greater detail and sophistication the nature of Japan's postwar national purpose. In the course of these negotiations he worked out a brilliant strategy—what we may call a Yoshida Doctrine—that served Japan for the next several decades. In his memoirs former secretary of state Henry Kissinger declared that "Japanese decisions have been the most farsighted and intelligent of any major nation of the postwar era."[5] This was Yoshida's achievement.

Opportunities in the Cold War. The critical moment for the determination of Japan's postwar orientation arrived in 1950 with the dangers and opportunities that the cold war rivalry offered Japan. The dangers were that Japan would be drawn into cold war politics, expend its limited and precious resources on remilitarization, and postpone the full economic and social recovery of its people. Conversely, Soviet-U.S. rivalry offered certain opportunities. The cold war made Japan strategically important to the United States and gave Yoshida bargaining leverage. He reasoned that Japan could make minimal concessions of passive cooperation with the Americans in return for an early end to the occupation, a long-term guarantee of its national security, and the opportunity to concentrate on all-out economic recovery.

In the early postwar days, the United States expected Japanese disarmament and neutrality to be supervised by the Allies for as long as twenty-five years to assure themselves and Japan's neighbors against Japanese remilitarization. By 1950 the onset of the cold war had changed the situation. The State Department was considering a regional defense alliance similar to NATO that would facilitate Japanese rearmament but keep it under international control. John Foster Dulles, special emissary of the secretary of state, envisioned a pact that would initially include the United States, Japan, Australia, New Zealand, the Philippines, and perhaps Indonesia. Such an alliance, permitted under Article 51 of the UN Charter, would internationalize Japanese forces, he reasoned, and thereby "ease reconciliation with the present . . . Constitution."[6] This arrangement, which would parallel the approach to the German question in Europe, is particularly interesting and significant since, as discussed in chapter 8, it remains an option today for drawing Japanese defense efforts into a multilateral context and thereby defusing the tensions in the bilateral security treaty, encouraging a more positive Japanese defense effort, and potentially allaying the concerns of Japan's neighbors. As Professor Ōtake Hideo has demonstrated, Yoshida's nationalism led him to reject this option of integration with neighboring Asian nations. In a pertinent observation, Ōtake writes: "Unlike Adenauer and Japanese leftist intellectuals, Yoshida never desired cultural or political integration of Japan with the West or with neighboring Asian nations. Although he was eager for international economic integration, he wished to maintain a distinctive cultural identity for the Japanese people. His sentimental attachment to the emperor must be understood in this context."[7]

Yoshida was not only unwilling to participate in a Pacific alliance system, he resisted all U.S. proposals to rebuild Japanese armed forces in response to the cold war. In retrospect, Yoshida clearly was determined to use the circumstances of the cold war to Japan's maximum advantage and to pursue a narrowly defined sense of national purpose. When Dulles came to Japan in June 1950 to negotiate a peace treaty and the end of the occupation, he urged Japanese rearmament. On this and subsequent occasions, Dulles sought to undo the MacArthur constitution by seeking the establishment of a large Japanese military force.

Yoshida, seizing the opportunity for what Nagai Yōnosuke calls "blackmail by the weak," refused to accede to these demands.[8] He established a bargaining position by making light of Japan's security problems and vaguely insisting that Japan could protect itself through its own devices by being democratic and peaceful and by relying on the protection of world opinion. After all, he argued, Japan had a constitution that, inspired by U.S. ideals and the lessons of defeat, renounced arms, and the Japanese people were determined to uphold it and to adhere to a new course in world affairs.

Yoshida's "puckish" and bravado performance left Dulles (in the words of a colleague) "flabbergasted," embittered, and feeling "very much like Alice in Wonderland."[9] In succeeding meetings, Yoshida negotiated from this position. He skillfully argued that rearmament would impoverish Japan and create the kind of social unrest that the Communists wanted. (We now know that through backdoor channels he was even prevailing on Socialist party leaders to whip up antirearmament demonstrations and campaigns during Dulles's visits!)[10] He further pointed out to Dulles the fears that other Asian countries had of a revived Japanese military, and he enlisted MacArthur's support. MacArthur obligingly urged that Japan remain a nonmilitary nation and instead contribute to the free world through its industrial production.[11] This happened in the Korean War. Yoshida's firmness spared Japan military involvement in the war and allowed it instead to profit enormously from procurement orders. Yoshida privately called the resulting stimulus to the economy "a gift of the gods." More such gifts appeared over the next decades.[12]

In the protracted negotiations with Dulles, Yoshida made minimal concessions; he consented to U.S. bases on Japanese soil and a limited rearmament, sufficient to gain Dulles's agreement to a peace treaty and to a postoccupation guarantee of Japanese security. The Yoshida Doctrine began to take shape in these negotiations. Its tenets were as follows:

1. Japan's economic rehabilitation must be the prime national goal. Political-economic cooperation with the United States was necessary for this purpose.

2. Japan should remain lightly armed and avoid involvement in international political-strategic issues. Not only would this low posture free the energies of its people for productive industrial development, it would avoid divisive internal struggles—what Yoshida called "a thirty-eighth parallel" in the hearts of the Japanese people.[13]

3. To gain a long-term guarantee for its own security, Japan would provide bases for the U.S. army, navy, and air force.*

---

*The appropriateness of the term "Yoshida Doctrine," which I use, can be debated. Professor Kōsaka Masataka has recorded that after he published an article in 1965 in *Chūō kōron* identifying Yoshida with a neomercantilist foreign policy, the latter rejected such an association. See Kōsaka, "The Quest for Credibility," *Look Japan*, September 10, 1981. Yoshida was too pragmatic and nondoctrinaire to allow his views to be characterized so simply. He himself never spoke of a "Yoshida Doctrine," and we can only conjecture at the ways he might have taken issue with the subsequent policies of the so-called Yoshida school. He was too proud and too much of a realist and nationalist to accept the implication of a politically and diplomatically passive Japan as a corollary of his policies. In an interesting exchange in 1984 between Nagai Yōnosuke, who also uses the term "Yoshida Doctrine," and Okazaki Hisahiko, the latter argued that postwar Japan has lacked any strategic doctrines. Nagai responded that the Yoshida Doctrine has been and will continue to be Japan's strategic doctrine, adding that just as Marx might not today be a Marxist, so it did not matter whether Yoshida was conscious of formulating a strategic doctrine:

NAGAI: "I call this [grand strategy] the 'Yoshida Doctrine.' Mr. Pyle of the University of Washington also uses the same term."

Yoshida's manipulation of both domestic politics and U.S. pressure was both shrewd and cynical. He made minimalist concessions to the U.S. demands for Japanese contribution to their own defense. Initially he offered military bases and a commitment to gradual rearmament. He grudgingly agreed to upgrade the National Police Reserve, which MacArthur established in July 1950 with 75,000 men, to the status of National Security Force in January 1952 with 110,000 men. At the same time, Yoshida warned the Americans of the necessity of improving living standards so as to forestall left-wing strength. Throughout, the Yoshida school had a shrewd awareness of U.S. ambivalence about Japan's rearmament: Yoshida and his successors were keenly aware that apprehension in the United States, as well as in Europe and Asia, about rearmament possibly going too far meant that demands for greater arms spending would always be tempered. The potential of a nationalist revival was therefore a brake on U.S. demands. In a comment highly revealing of his method, Yoshida told a young associate (a future prime minister), Miyazawa Kiichi, at the time that

> the day [for rearmament] will come naturally when our livelihood recovers. It may sound devious (*zurui*), but let the Americans handle [our security] until then. It is indeed our Heaven-bestowed good fortune that the Constitution bans arms. If the Americans complain, the Constitution gives us a perfect justification. The politicians who want to amend it are fools.[14]

Yoshida, in short, was convinced that the cold war would require the United States to maintain its presence in Japan, which alone would be sufficient to deter a Soviet attack. He would therefore give exclusive priority to pursuing Japanese economic recovery and maintaining political stability and would defer indefinitely the task of preparing the Japanese people themselves for a return to the hard realities of international politics. It became an

---

OKAZAKI: "Yes, but Mr. Pyle clearly states in his writing that Yoshida himself declared that there was no such thing."

NAGAI: "That makes no difference. . . . What Yoshida Shigeru really thought has absolutely no relation to the 'Yoshida Doctrine.' "

See Okazaki Hisahiko and Nagai Yōnosuke, "Nani ga senryakuteki riarizumu ka," *Chūō kōron*, July 1984.

idée fixe of postwar Japanese diplomacy to avoid any collective security commitments. The constitution gave a convenient pretext for a narrow self-interested foreign policy. Unlike Konrad Adenauer, to whom he is often compared and who wanted German integration into Europe, Yoshida was too much of a nationalist to favor anything but economic ties with Asia.

His resistance to Dulles's pressure for participation in a regional collective security arrangement, however, had its price. On the same day that the San Francisco Peace Treaty was signed (September 8, 1951), a security treaty was also signed with the United States that was highly unequal, preserved many of the occupation prerogatives of the U.S. military, and in effect rendered Japan a military satellite of the United States. In addition to granting bases to the United States, it gave the United States a veto over any third country's military presence in Japan, the right to intervene to quell domestic disorder in Japan, the right to project military power from bases in Japan against a third country without consulting Japan, and an indefinite time period for the treaty. In addition, the United States insisted on extraterritorial legal rights for its military and dependents. At the same time, Yoshida was also compelled to recognize Taiwan as the legitimate government of China and thus forswear normal relations with the mainland government. In sum, Dulles exacted a heavy price from Yoshida for his stubborn refusal to participate in a regional collective security alliance.

Later Regrets. There is now substantial evidence that Yoshida, in his last years, after he had left office, came to regret the course that he set for the nation at this critical juncture. He seemed implicitly to acknowledge the dissembling and cynical ways in which he had used Article 9 as a pretext and ploy to evade American pressure to participate in its own defense. Yoshida wrote to a colleague that "the renewal of national strength and development of political independence require that Japan possess a military force as a matter of national honor," and he confessed to "deep feelings of responsibility over the present situation on the national defense issue."[15] He further wrote in 1963, nearly a decade after leaving office:

> In my recent travels, I have met with leaders of other countries who have recovered from war and are contributing to world peace and prosperity. I feel Japan should be contributing too. For an independent Japan, which is

among the first rank countries in economics, technology, and learning, to continue to be dependent on another country is a deformity (*katawa*) of the state. . . . For Japan, a member of the United Nations and expecting its benefits, to avoid support of its peacekeeping mechanisms is selfish behavior. This is unacceptable in international society. I myself cannot escape responsibility for the use of the Constitution as a pretext (*tatemae*) for this way of conducting national policy.[16]

Yoshida was sensitive to the association of his name with the neomercantilist role of Japan. In a 1964 article in *Chūō kōron*, entitled "Japan as a Maritime Nation," one of Yoshida's scholarly admirers and one of the country's most influential political scientists, Kōsaka Masataka, defined Japan's national purpose as that of a great trading nation, like Venice or the Netherlands in the past, and traced its origins to Yoshida:

Japan's postwar involvement with the West . . . has been primarily economic rather than military, an emphasis chosen by Prime Minister Yoshida Shigeru at the time of Japan's negotiations with America over the 1951 San Francisco Peace Treaty. Yoshida believed that economic matters are more important than military, and, for this reason, he rejected America's suggestion that Japan rearm and spearhead American military strategy in the Far East. Japan's foreign policy has subsequently been simply a kind of "neomercantilism." . . . Yoshida's choice has proved a most adequate one for Japan. From a strictly military point of view, Japan's "neomercantilist" diplomacy has been adequate for two reasons: First, the development of nuclear weapons has greatly lessened the ethical justification as well as the effectiveness of military power. Second, since Japan has been fully protected by the U.S. Seventh Fleet, in terms of defense her own rearmament would have been superfluous. From a political point of view, Yoshida's "neomercantilism" has harmonized with Japan's postwar democratization.[17]

Kōsaka later recorded that Yoshida read this article and flatly rejected identification of his name with neomercantilism: "He told me there could be no such policy."[18] Yoshida's inbred nationalism was repelled by the implication of a politically and diplomatically passive Japan as a corollary of his policies. At the time, however, he acknowledged responsibility for the path taken.

Resisting U.S. Pressure. U.S. pressure on Japan to participate more actively in its alliance system resumed shortly after the signing of the peace and security treaties. In October 1951 Congress passed the Mutual Security Assistance (MSA) Act, which was designed "to consolidate the American alliance system through the supply of weapons and equipment, participation of allied officers in training programs in the United States, and the overall coordination of military strategies."[19] The efforts of the Americans to persuade Japan to participate in this more intimate military relationship called forth another bravado performance by Yoshida in which he sought to gain the economic benefits of the relationship and to avoid the strategic obligations.

The United States pressed Japan to accept military aid for a threefold expansion of its forces from the 110,000-man National Security Force to an army of 350,000. Yoshida knew that increasing the size of the army, besides being controversial at home, would bring closer the day when the United States would press Japan to dispatch it for overseas conflict in the cold war. He was instinctively hostile to participation in the arrangement, but he also sensed the possibility of economic benefits. Japanese business was considerably interested because the end of the procurement orders as the Korean War wound down had contributed to declining economic prospects. Business leaders saw the possibilities of further economic aid for reconstruction, acquisition of advanced technology, and improved industrial competitiveness.[20] The defense committee (*Bōei seisan iinkai*) of Keidanren (Federation of Economic Organizations) with backing from the Ministry of International Trade and Industry (MITI), hoped to build up Japan's weapons industry with U.S. help and thus to promote exports and to acquire the spinoff effect of advanced technologies.

Clearly Yoshida again set out to contain U.S. pressure for military obligations and to use MSA aid for economic reconstruction and development. Yoshida depended heavily on his protege, Ikeda Hayato, the former minister of finance, to negotiate with the United States and to make as few concessions as possible on rearmament. Given the enormous pressure that Dulles and the U.S. government brought to bear, Yoshida had to expand the National Security Force to preserve a satisfactory relationship with the United States. Nonetheless, Yoshida's sharply honed sense of national purpose once again succeeded in limiting Japan's obligations.

The MSA agreement that Japan and the United States signed in March 1954, while acknowledging again (as in the security treaty) that "Japan will itself increasingly assume responsibility for its own defense," at the same time emphasized that "Japan can only contribute to the extent permitted by its general economic conditions" and acknowledged that "the present Agreement will be implemented by each Government in accordance with the constitutional provisions of the respective countries." At the signing ceremonies Okazaki Katsuo, the Japanese foreign minister, said: "There are no new and separate military duties. Overseas service and so on for Japan's internal security force will not arise."[21] Japan was also able to direct substantial MSA assistance into economic development, helping to overcome the economic stagnation that set in as the Korean War ended. Nagai Yōnosuke sees this contest between Yoshida and the Americans over MSA aid as a turning point: if Japan had moved toward a military-industrial emphasis in tandem with the Americans, "there would have been no Japanese economic miracle."[22]

In the month the MSA agreement was signed, the Japanese government, complying with the demands brought by Washington in connection with the MSA agreement, introduced legislation to reorganize and to expand the armed forces, including an air force. Even while providing the legal basis of Japan's subsequent military organization, Yoshida was able to temper U.S. demands in significant ways. In 1954, the Defense Agency Establishment Law and the Self-Defense Forces Law created the National Defense Agency (Bōeichō) with responsibility for ground, maritime, and air self-defense forces with a total of 152,000 men—substantially less than half of what the United States had demanded. Moreover, the upper house of the Diet at the same time passed a unanimous resolution opposing the dispatch of forces overseas on constitutional and other grounds, a position the government had previously asserted on many occasions in the Diet. So narrow and self-centered was Japan's sense of national purpose, U.S. Ambassador John Allison concluded that "Japan has no basic convictions for or against the free world." Dulles, once again frustrated by Yoshida's intransigence on the rearmament issue, confessed himself "grievously disappointed" that there was "no revival in Japan of the spirit of sacrifice and discipline" or "great national spirit."[23]

Yoshida's Retirement. Yoshida's skill in manipulating his left-wing and conservative opponents finally failed him when they turned on him for accumulated grievances and forced his retirement in December 1954. As Ōtake writes, "Although Yoshida's policy contributed to rapid economic recovery by minimizing national security costs and at the same time keeping the alliance tolerable for Washington, it frustrated the rightists and increased the suspicion of the leftists, eventually leading to wide party cleavages on defense controversies."[24] Yoshida was replaced by conservative opponents who were frankly political nationalists and who chafed at his economics-first policies. They governed from 1955 to 1960 with a wholly different approach to foreign policy. They wanted to revise the constitution, to carry out a forthright rearmament, to negotiate a more equal security treaty with the United States, and generally to pursue a more autonomous and independent course.

This agenda, which could have succeeded in 1950 if Yoshida had supported it, encountered greater obstacles in the latter half of the 1950s. The left wing of the Japan Socialist party (JSP) was now firmly in control of the party and passionately committed to an ideological defense of the constitution and a neutralist foreign policy. In addition, Yoshida, now out of power, sabotaged the efforts to achieve an independent foreign policy stance by raising doubts in Washington about his successor's negotiations with the Soviets to achieve a peace treaty. With a Japanese conservative government that was bent on revising the constitution in power, Washington had an opportunity to achieve the kind of response on rearmament that it had long sought, but at the same time it was suspicious of Tokyo's independent course. In any case, the JSP had gained sufficient strength in the Diet, and its hold on public opinion through the media, intellectuals, and the unions made constitutional revision much more difficult.

The two countries did, however, move to revise the security treaty. Kishi Nobusuke, an anti-Yoshida conservative who served as prime minister from 1957 to 1960, wanted to eliminate the unequal aspects of the existing treaty; as long as dispatch of Japanese troops overseas and participation in collective defense were interpreted as unconstitutional, however, a completely equal and reciprocal treaty was impossible. Nonetheless, the anti-Yoshida conservatives wanted to eliminate the clause permitting U.S. intervention in domestic disturbances, they wanted a voice in the deployment of U.S. forces stationed in Japan, and they wanted a fixed term for the treaty and an explicit guarantee of U.S. protection in case of an attack. Kishi, who had served in the Tōjō cabinet and had been indicted as a war criminal during the occupation, aroused widespread distrust. The JSP mounted a fierce public opposition to ratification of the new security treaty, which was signed in 1960. Ratification was rammed through the Diet, but Kishi's administration ended with the greatest mass demonstrations in Japanese history.

This tumultuous outcome of the insistence by anti-Yoshida

conservatives on raising the divisive issues of constitutional revision and rearmament gave a long-term advantage to the Yoshida school. The demonstrations of 1960 showed the popular strength of the opposition; the continued preoccupation of many conservatives with these issues would subject the country to prolonged turmoil. For the next two decades, rather than weaken political stability, these divisive issues were shelved, and the conservatives turned again to the Yoshida wing of the party, which was acknowledged to be the mainstream.

Institutionalization of the Yoshida Doctrine

Under the next two prime ministers, Ikeda Hayato (1960–1964) and Satō Eisaku (1964–1972), both closely associated with Yoshida, the Yoshida Doctrine was institutionalized and consolidated into a national consensus. Ikeda, who had been Yoshida's key economic adviser and finance minister, suppressed the divisive issues of political nationalism and instead adopted a political strategy of a low posture toward the Socialists intended to establish stability and policies of managed economic growth. Both Ikeda and Satō ignored the recommendation of their party's Research Committee for Constitutional Revision, which favored repeal of Article 9.

Economic Nationalism. Working with his economic adviser, Osamu Shimomura, and the heads of the Economic Planning Agency, the Ministry of Finance, and the Ministry of International Trade and Industry, Ikeda formulated a plan for doubling the national income within a decade. This plan, which actually had its origins in the Kishi administration but had been sidetracked by the priority given to the security treaty, was part of a systematic and well-coordinated effort to formulate policies that would steer clear of ideology, raise living standards, and improve social overhead capital. It added up to an exclusive concentration on issues of economic nationalism on which the Liberal Democratic party, (LDP), the bureaucracy, the political opposition, and the populace generally could achieve substantial agreement. Almost imperceptibly the appeal of the political Left was coopted, and the country settled down to a long period of enthusiastic pursuit of high-growth policies. Nakamura Takafusa, one of the leading historians of Japan's postwar economy, writes that

> Ikeda was the single most important figure in Japan's
> rapid growth. He should be remembered as the man who

pulled together a national consensus for economic growth and who strove for the realization of the goal. . . . From a broader perspective, however, Japan consistently adhered to Yoshida Shigeru's view that armaments should be curbed and military spending suppressed while all efforts were concentrated on the reconstruction of the economy.[25]

Under another Yoshida protege, Satō Eisaku, who succeeded Ikeda and held the prime ministership longer (1964–1972) than any other individual in Japanese history, the Yoshida Doctrine was further elaborated in terms of nuclear-strategic issues. In 1967 Satō enunciated the three nonnuclear principles, which helped to calm pacifist fears aroused by China's nuclear experiments and the escalation of the war in Vietnam. The three principles held that Japan would not produce, possess, or permit the introduction of nuclear weapons onto its soil. Lest the principles be regarded as unconditional, Satō clarified matters in a Diet speech the following year in which he described the four pillars of Japan's nonnuclear policy: (1) reliance on the U.S. nuclear umbrella, (2) the three nonnuclear principles, (3) promotion of worldwide disarmament, and (4) development of nuclear energy for peaceful purposes. In short, the U.S. nuclear umbrella was to be the sine qua non of the nonnuclear principles. Satō was awarded the Nobel Peace Prize, but detractors like the prominent economist Tsuru Shigeto, who wanted an unconditional declaration, called it hypocrisy to proclaim nonnuclearism while taking shelter under another country's nuclear umbrella.

In 1967 Satō added another building block to the structure of foreign policy that Yoshida had begun. To defuse domestic political turmoil and to preserve Japan's low posture in international politics, he formulated the policy of the three principles of arms exports (buki yushutsu san-gensoku), which provided that Japan would not allow the export of arms to countries in the Communist bloc, to countries covered by UN resolutions on arms embargoes, and to countries involved or likely to be involved in armed conflicts. Subsequently the Miki cabinet (1974–1976) extended this ban on weapons exports to all countries and defined "arms" to include not only military equipment but also the parts and fittings used in this equipment.

As a further refinement to the policy, constraining defense expenditures to less than 1 percent of the gross national product became a practice in the 1960s, although it did not become official government policy until adoption of the National Defense Program Outline in 1976. The outline contained a provision that "in maintaining the armed strength, the total amount of defense expenditure in each fiscal year shall not exceed, for the time being, an amount equivalent to 1/100th of the gross national product of the said fiscal year."

Avoiding Security Obligations. By the time Satō became prime minister in the mid-1960s, the Yoshida Doctrine had been institutionalized and had become a national consensus. Yoshida's policies had taken on a life of their own. Not only had they proved their worth as a strategy for maintaining domestic political stability and securing LDP rule, but they were successful in keeping the Americans at bay. The antitreaty demonstrations gave proof of the strength of popular resistance to greater defense efforts and the dangers of socialist upheaval; the Kennedy and Johnson administrations were content to give priority to Japanese economic development as a means to ensure Japan's stability and democratic development. The State Department, with the aid of the embassy in Tokyo headed by Ambassador Reischauer, drafted a secret policy paper on the future of Japan in 1964 which urged support of Japan's economic goals and recommended "firm Executive Branch resistance of American industry demands for curtailment of Japanese imports."[26]

The Vietnam conflict, however, renewed U.S. determination to increase the Japanese contribution to Asian security. Particularly during the Nixon administration the issue was again raised of Japan's role in the collective security of Asia in connection with the possible return of Okinawa and more broadly the Nixon Doctrine, which declared that the United States would depend on its Asian allies to assume more of the responsibility for containing communism in the region. But the Japanese by this time were overwhelmingly opposed to direct involvement in regional security organizations. Such a role, said former foreign minister Ōhira, a long-time associate of Ikeda, was "impossible."[27]

The sharp-tongued Sonoda Sunao, another former foreign minister, revealed the cynical approach that often lay behind the conservative elite's approach to U.S. efforts to enlist Japanese cooperation in maintaining Asian security. Sonoda, a nationalist who had opposed the security treaty, told an Australian political scientist with heavy sarcasm that Japanese efforts to elude American attempts to engage them in collective security arrangements were a constant of Japanese foreign policy:

> The Americans were always asking us to do this and to do that, to take over part of the burden of their Far Eastern policies. But all their efforts were sabotaged by one Japanese Cabinet after another. That's why Satō Eisaku got the Nobel Peace Prize. He got it for his accumulated achievements in the field of sabotage. I suppose he is the only Prime Minister ever to have got the Nobel Peace Prize for sabotage.[28]

While South Korea dispatched more than 300,000 troops to fight alongside the Americans, the Japanese avoided direct military involvement. At the same time, "the Japanese procurements industry, stagnant since the end of the Korea War, entered a new period of rapid expansion. Profits were staggering. In the late 1960s Washington's annual military expenditure in Japan was almost invariably larger than its expenditure in Vietnam itself."[29]

During the 1960s and 1970s, Yoshida's successors offered many formulations of both defense and foreign policy that sought to maintain Japan's low political profile and the broad consensus for pursuit of the economics-first policy. One frequently cited concept was "an exclusively defensive defense" (senshu bōei): troops and weapons would have no offensive capacity. According to this, jets would have no capability for bombing or midair refueling. The concept of "comprehensive security" (sōgō anzen hoshō) tried to redefine security to include overseas aid and disaster relief. Kōsaka Masataka, a leading conservative theorist, admitted, "Though excellent in theory [a comprehensive security capability] has actually been an excuse, even a lie, to avoid greater defense efforts."[30] Guided by its "omni-directional foreign policy" (zenhōi gaikō), which was invoked during oil crises, Japan should maintain cordial relations with all countries to ensure supplies of energy and raw materials and to protect trade.

As Matsuoka Hideo, a foreign affairs commentator who later ran for governor of Tokyo, wrote in 1980, Japan should continue to avoid becoming entangled in international disputes by deliberately "missing the boat" (nori-okure); that is, when international issues arose, Japan should always "go to the end of the line" and wait quietly, unnoticed, while all other nations stepped forward to declare their positions on controversial issues. This passive and reactive policy, he admitted, was a "diplomacy of cowardice" (okubyō gaikō), but it served Japan's interests of maintaining good relations with all countries and thus preserving its global access to markets and raw materials. "No matter where or what kind of dispute or war arises," he concluded, "Japan must stand aloof and uninvolved."[31]

One Yoshida disciple, Miyazawa Kiichi, who served as foreign minister in the 1970s and became prime minister in 1991, summed up Japanese foreign policy as a "value-free diplomacy," which sought to avoid ideological conflict with left-wing progressive forces in Japanese politics by "separating economics from politics."[32] In maintaining this broad consensus for the pursuit of economic growth, the Yoshida school not only avoided political confrontation, it often preempted popular progressive causes. A good example was Satō's 1969 initiative to establish the United Nations University in Tokyo.

As the Yoshida Doctrine demonstrated its success, the consensus became deeply rooted, almost instinctual. Every country has its share of sophistry in its foreign policy rationales, but in the Japanese case the gap between pretense and reality was extreme. A former senior MITI official, Amaya Naohiro, observed, "Postwar Japan defined itself as a cultural state holding the principles of liberalism, democracy and peace, but these were only superficial principles (*tatemae*); the fundamental objective (*honne*) was the pouring of all our strength into economic growth."[33] The U.S. preoccupation with the cold war, the writer Nishio Kanji confessed, allowed Japan to "conduct a diplomacy that exploited and totally used the U.S. Even if Japan was asked to take some responsibility, we could get away with avoiding it and simply pursue our own economic interests."[34] The success of this narrowly self-interested approach to foreign policy led to a fixed belief that a low-posture, inconspicuous role was the key to success.

Supporters of the Mercantilist Role. By 1980 the confidence that a mercantilist role in international affairs best suited Japanese national interests was widely accepted in the mainstream of the political, bureaucratic, and business elites. The leading conservative theorist Kōsaka Masataka wrote in his 1981 book *Bunmei ga suibō suru toki* that Japan should continue to act the role of a merchant in the world community—a middleman taking advantage of commercial relations and avoiding involvement in international politics. "A trading nation (*tsūshō kokka*) does not go to war," he wrote.

> Neither does it make supreme efforts to bring peace. It simply takes advantage of international relations created by stronger nations. This can also be said of our economic activities. In the most basic sense, we do not create

things. We live by purchasing primary products and semifinished products and processing them. That is to say, we live by utilizing other people's production.[35]

Kōsaka emphasized that this was not a popular role in the international order since it was regarded as selfish and even immoral. It caused problems, particularly with the United States, because "Japan has enjoyed the advantages of being an ally and the benefits of noninvolvement." With the breakdown of the Bretton Woods system and the oil crisis, Kōsaka foresaw difficult times as "politics and economics become more intertwined in the economic policies of nations."

Kōsaka believed that Japan could adapt to the new circumstances and survive as a trading nation if it could manage its crisis of spirit. That is, in holding firmly to no clear principles but merely pursuing commercial advantage, the danger was that the Japanese might lose self-respect. All trading nations, he wrote, face this crisis.

A trading nation has wide relations with many alien civilizations, making differing use of various different principles of behavior, and manages to harmonize them with each other. This, however, tends to weaken the self-confidence and identity of the persons engaged in the operation. They gradually come to lose sight of what they really value and even of who they really are.

To deal with this psychological burden, trading nations, he concluded, "need the confidence that they are contributing to the world in their own way. Only by doing so does hypocrisy (*gizen*) cease to be hypocrisy for hypocrisy's sake. It becomes a relatively harmless method of doing good."[36]

Amaya Naohiro was one of the most outspoken and flamboyant advocates of the merchant role. In a series of widely discussed articles marked by their color and candor and written while he was serving as MITI's vice minister for international affairs, Amaya drew analogies from Japanese history to illustrate the role of a merchant nation, which he hoped Japan would pursue in a consistent and thoroughgoing manner. He likened international society to Tokugawa Japan, when society was divided into four functional classes: samurai, peasants, artisans, and merchants. The United States and the Soviet Union fulfilled the roles of samurai, whereas Japan based itself on commerce and industry; third world countries were peasant societies. If the military role of the samurai were not exercised, as happened in the Tokugawa period, then it might be possible to conclude that "the world exists for Japan," but in fact international society was a jungle, and the merchant must act with great circumspection. The nation for some time had conducted itself like an international trading firm, he wrote, but it had not wholeheartedly acknowledged this role and pursued it single-mindedly.

Amaya wanted the Japanese to show the ability, shrewdness, and self-discipline of the sixteenth-century merchant princes of Hakata and Sakai, whose adroit maneuvering in the midst of a samurai-dominated society allowed them to prosper. "In the sixteenth-century world of turmoil and warfare, they accepted their difficult destiny, living unarmed or with only light arms. To tread this path, they put aside all illusions, overcame the temptation of dependency (*amae no kōzō*), and concentrated on calmly dealing with reality." By the end of the Tokugawa period, Amaya pointed out, merchants were so powerful that Honda Toshiaki (1744–1821) remarked, "In appearance all of Japan belongs to the samurai, but in reality it is owned by the merchants." What was required was to stay the course, to put aside the samurai's pride of principle. "For a merchant to prosper in samurai society, it is necessary to have superb information-gathering ability, planning ability, intuition, diplomatic skill, and at times ability to be a sycophant (*gomasuri nōryoku*)."

In Amaya's view, pride and principle should not stand in the way of the pursuit of profit:

> From now on if Japan chooses to live as a merchant nation (*chōnin kokka*) in international society, I think it is important that it pursue wholeheartedly the way of the merchant. When necessary, it must beg for oil from the producing countries; sometimes it must grovel on bended knee before the samurai.

The Tokugawa merchant was not above using his wealth to gain his way, and Amaya counseled that Japan similarly must be prepared to buy solutions to its political problems: "When money can help, it is important to have the gumption to put up large sums."[37]

An international incident with Amaya himself at the center attracted attention to the psychological costs of behaving in the manner he prescribed. Following the seizure of the U.S. Embassy in Teheran in November 1979, the U.S. government sought the cooperation of its allies in applying sanctions against Iran. Japan, seeking to protect its oil imports from Iran and to avoid involve-

ment in the dispute, responded ambiguously. When it was revealed, however, that Japanese companies were continuing to
make large purchases of Iranian oil, the samurai nation was angry.
Secretary of State Cyrus Vance met with Foreign Minister Ōkita
Saburō and sharply criticized Japanese insensitivity; twelve U.S.
senators introduced a resolution criticizing Japan; and U.S. news-
papers expressed outrage. It was time for the merchant nation to
make its response. Amaya, who was in Washington representing
MITI, called a formal press conference to apologize and to assure
Americans that Japanese companies would "behave themselves
and never repeat such misbehavior." This indeed smacked of the
merchant's "ability to be a sycophant."

The Yoshida strategy was not only firmly rooted in political,
bureaucratic, and business elite thinking by the 1980s, it had also
been translated into a strategic doctrine. One of Japan's leading
political strategists, Nagai Yōnosuke, wrote that the merchant role
possessed extraordinary durability not only because of the strong
domestic coalition of forces that supported it but also because it
suited Japan's strategic needs in the existing international system.
In 1981, he wrote:

> Despite the questionable nature of its origins, the new
> constitution has weathered thirty-five years, has been
> assimilated to Japanese traditions and culture, and, in a
> word, has been Japanized. In my judgment, the Japanese
> people will refuse ever again to become a state in the
> traditional sense but will choose to exist as a kind of
> "moratorium state."

Nagai believed that "the incongruity of status" (*chii no hiikkansei*)
between Japan's great economic power and the modest development of its political strength was appropriate to the Japanese
national interest in a world dominated by nuclear weapons.[38]

A "Moratorium State." Nagai set forth a concept of what he called
the "moratorium world" and of Japan as a "moratorium state"
(*moratoriamu kokka*). He described world politics as in a state of
transition from the traditional international order (the Westphalian
system) in which the status of nation-states was established according to their military power, to what he called a Kantian,
peaceful world order in which the security of states would be
preserved by a collective international arrangement. This transition stage was marked by a nuclear standoff or parity between the
superpowers, which had created a power moratorium in the

world. As a consequence, military power counted for less in determining the hierarchy of nations; international economic strength and technological know-how counted for more. In other words, in this moratorium world there was no longer a single agreed-on measure of status among nations: one state might have great military power; another might have great economic strength. There was no reason that the status of a state must be congruent on all attributes.

Therefore the incongruity between Japan's economic power and political-military weakness was not odd but reflected the nature of this new situation. Demands on Japan to maintain a military establishment consistent with its economic standing, wrote Nagai in 1981, reflected a projection onto the world community of a drive in Western society to achieve consistency in personal status. Japanese, however, were accustomed to inconsistency of status, as shown by the Tokugawa system: samurai had political power and prestige, while the merchants had economic power. In a passage reminiscent of Amaya's thesis, Nagai quoted Yamaga Sokō (1622–1685): "Samurai live by honor, whereas farmers, artisans, and merchants live by interest." Moreover, among the samurai there was a complex allocation of different roles. Among the feudal lords, for example, the *tozama* were given great territorial domains but no place in the central government; the *fudai* had administrative power but little territory. The purpose of this complex system was "to prevent the centralization of power by the drive to achieve consistency of status, which is a weakness of all men." What was necessary for the advancement of human society was the "globalization of the Tokugawa system," by which Nagai appeared to envision a complex system of checks and balances in which different nations fulfilled different roles.

The future of Japan, for Nagai, was as a moratorium state; that is, in light of the current state of international politics, Japan should preserve its present constitution and "maintain the inconsistency in its status as a lightly armed, nonnuclear economic power." Strategic planning should concentrate on a limited but highly sophisticated defense posture, depending on advanced high technology such as lasers, precision-guided missiles, radar, and the like. Diplomacy should preserve the U.S.-Japan Mutual Security Treaty and seek economic cooperation with the Soviet Union so that the latter had no cause for hostilities against Japan. Should the United States increase its pressure on Japan, presumably on economic or defense issues, or should the Soviet Union build up its power unduly in the Far East, Japan always had the potential threat of a nationalist response: revision of the constitution, conversion of its industry and technology to military purposes, development of nuclear weapons, and so on. This threat gave Japan bargaining power to preserve its posture.

By the 1980s the Yoshida Doctrine had become a finely tuned policy for dealing with the foreign and domestic issues that engaged Japan's conservative elite. Within Japan, the Yoshida Doctrine maintained a balance between those groups concerned with security even at the expense of national pride and those concerned with preservation of national autonomy and sovereignty. Keenly aware of Japan's political-economic vulnerability, it balanced security and economic concerns. Moreover, within the bureaucracy the Yoshida Doctrine came to represent a balancing of bureaucratic conflicts among the Ministry of Finance, MITI, the Ministry of Foreign Affairs, and the Defense Agency. Professor Igarashi Takeshi refers to it as a "domestic foreign policy *system*" because of the way in which the foreign policies of the opposition groups were accommodated.[39] The Yoshida Doctrine was a political compromise between the pacifism of opposition groups and the security concerns of the right-wing conservatives. There has been what appears to be tantamount to a tacit agreement with socialist and pacifist groups that divisive issues of constitutional revision and substantial military spending would be moderated and priority given to economic growth and social welfare. In managing both domestic politics and Japan's international relations, it seemed to work so well that Nagai Yōnosuke wrote in 1985, "The Yoshida Doctrine will be permanent (*eien de aru*)."[40]

4

Competing Views of Japanese Purpose

In the summer of 1945, as the last days of the war unfolded, Ryū Shintarō, a correspondent for the *Asahi* in Europe, wrote to a friend in the Japanese cabinet that Japan must resolve to end the fighting and to embark on a new course so that Japan could rise again "in fifty years in a new form."[1] The Pax Americana after 1945 provided a liberal international economic order in which a defeated and outcast nation could take refuge, focus its sights on economic growth, and seek to rise again in such a new form. Relying on the U.S.'s preoccupation with the cold war to provide Japan with security and an open market, Japan intensified its bureaucratic controls and strengthened its mercantilist policies. Reversing many occupation reforms and rebuilding many illiberal political-economic institutions, the country redoubled its efforts in a more concentrated economic rather than political struggle. As two Japanese economists described it, "the banks and the economic bureaucracy functioned as a general staff behind the battlefield in this second 'total war' (*dai-ni sōryokusen*) called high economic growth."[2] Thus Yoshida and his successors determined to profit from the international order even while flouting its liberal norms. Economic nationalism became, as Matsumoto Sannosuke observed, "an apolitical way of 'enhancing the international prestige,' replacing the prewar approach based on military power."[3] The technical skills once applied to building military power were turned to economic ends for a similar purpose of overtaking the Western powers. As one diplomat reminisced in 1979:

The [mighty battleship] *Yamato* and the Zeros—forerunners of the postwar Japanese technology—are still very much alive, so it is said among us Japanese, in mammoth tankers, excellent automotive engines, etc., which Japan turns out by the thousands and millions. Thus they have served our nation in a manner never foreseen in their heyday.[4]

Quasi-wartime controls were implemented to close off the financial system to the rest of the world; economic strategy was devised with a military tactical sense that was often reflected in the terminology used. The Finance Ministry's tight regulatory controls over Japanese banks were likened to "the escort of a convoy of ships by a warship."[5] The efforts of the Japanese people were regimented toward saving rather than consumption; support of the nation's export-oriented productive capacity through concentration of resources and economies of scale took precedence over economic democracy. As one MITI official stressed in 1962:

Free competition has a stifling effect on the economy. We must not allow it to be used in distributing the benefits of high growth—prices, wages, profits. . . . We cannot pause to theorize about the sort of influence that a policy of concentration will have. If our export strength is assured, the growth of our economy is assured.[6]

More than any other country, Japan was the beneficiary of the postwar international order. For more than a quarter of a century after the end of World War II, Japan operated in extraordinary and uniquely favorable political-economic circumstances. In contrast to every other major power, it was spared the psychological and material costs of participating in international politics. Accordingly, the Japanese were able to concentrate their resources and their energies on achieving economic growth. Until the late 1960s, Japan benefited from a special relationship with the United States under which the latter sponsored Japanese recovery and development by keeping the U.S. market open to Japan's goods while allowing Japan to limit severely access to its own economy. The expanding world trade that the United States was promoting through regimes of the International Monetary Fund (IMF) and the General Agreement on Tariffs and Trade (GATT) permitted a vigorous expansion of Japanese manufactured goods and the ready purchase of abundant and cheap raw materials. Moreover, Japan had easy access to new, inexpensive, and more efficient Western technology, which it imported in large quantities. As one intelligent observer, Kōsaka Masataka, commented, "The international environment of the 1960s looked as though Heaven (*ten*) had created it for Japan's economic growth."[7]

The Yoshida Doctrine proved much more durable than its author anticipated because of its effectiveness in dealing with the international as well as the domestic political environment. As Japanese economic recovery gave way to high economic growth, the doctrine took on a life of its own, continually proving its effectiveness by the achievements that took place in the economy and the relative stability it was able to maintain at home. To the progressives, economic success confirmed their contention that Japan could thrive without arms. But success also gave rise to renewed pride in Japanese cultural values, which was often at odds with the radicalism of the progressives. In addition, success prompted a new nationalist mood in the land that was fed by writers urging a more assertive political role in the world. The Yoshida school, which was the mainstream of the conservative party, navigated skillfully between the contending views of the progressives and the political nationalists, often coopting elements of their agendas to maintain the consensus of Japanese purpose.

Progressive View of Japanese Purpose

While the nexus of business-government-bureaucracy quietly pursued its policies of economic nationalism, Japan conveyed a different sense of its national purpose to the world. This was the world view offered by the progressive forces. It proclaimed Japan as a nation transformed by its experience of war, atomic bombings, and defeat, dedicated to showing the way to a new world in which nations would exist free of weapons and not resort to war. This view, enshrined in the constitution and the fundamental reforms imposed by the occupation, was the face Japan most often showed to the world. It was the ideology taught in the schools; it was the rationale offered internationally for Japanese foreign policy; it served to legitimate the abstention from collective security arrangements even while Japan depended on the international order for its growing prosperity; it was the stuff of UN speeches by Japanese prime ministers.

The progressives, which in the 1960s included the most articulate segment of Japanese opinion, drew their support from the media, intellectuals, teachers, students, labor unions, white-collar workers, opposition parties, and certain religious groups. Theirs was a vision of Japan as a peace state (*heiwa kokka*) and of the Japanese as a resocialized people with a unique mission to show the way to a new world in which disputes would be resolved without resort to arms.

The finest hour of the progressives was the postwar reform era. Their ideas emerged out of the wartime disillusion, revulsion from Japanese nationalism, and profound distrust of traditional state power. They embraced the universalist pretensions of the new institutions established by the occupation. Progressives held that prewar nationalism, which had been built on extraordinary claims of the collectivist ethic, the Japanese family-state, and the emperor system, had led them astray. Particularism had blinded them to their real self-interest, had overcome their best instincts, and had reduced them to international outcasts. How better to redeem themselves in the eyes of the world than by turning their backs on the particular claims of nationality and proclaiming themselves citizens of the world. Therefore, not only did they embrace liberal values and institutions; they were enthusiastically swept up in the mystique of a noble experiment. They would even renounce the usual claims of sovereignty, "trusting," as the preamble of the constitution declared, "in the peace-loving peoples of the world."

Progressives took their stand in support of the new postwar democratic order and above all in support of the role that the constitution envisioned for Japan in the world. Progressives argued that Japan's unique mission in the postwar world was to demonstrate that a modern industrial nation could exist without arming itself, that Japan could show the way to a new world in which national sovereignty would be forsworn. Nation-states, which were artificial creations, would disappear, allowing the naturally harmonious impulses of the world's societies to usher in a peaceful international order. The Japanese people, having been victimized by a reactionary leadership that indoctrinated them in an artificial nationalism, had shown the demented course of the modern nation-state by its aggressions in Asia. As victims of the advent of atomic weapons, the Japanese people could convincingly argue that wars were ever more destructive, that a new age in international affairs was accordingly at hand, and that the sovereign prerogative to go to war must be renounced. No other nation embraced the liberal hope for the future world order with the enthusiasm of Japan, for no other nation's recent experiences seemed to bear out so compellingly the costs of the old ways. This view had deep and profound appeal. It provided a new orientation, an idealistic mission that would expiate Japan's sins. More-over, it provided a justification for rejecting world politics and devoting national energies entirely to rebuilding the national livelihood.

The mainstream conservatives of the Yoshida school dealt effectively with the progressives' competing view of Japanese national purpose partly by dismissing their conception as utopian and un-Japanese and partly by coopting some elements of their view. Elements of the progressive vision were incorporated into the Yoshida strategy, as evidenced by the resistance to all-out armament, the abstention from power politics, and the rejection of nuclear weapons. Above all, the Yoshida Doctrine, although aligning Japan with the United States in the cold war, steadfastly resisted being drawn into any collective security obligations that would have inflamed the progressives.

In domestic affairs, the conservatives played a skillful hand, following "centrist policies designed to dampen the potential Left-Right confrontation inherent in postwar Japan and to establish and maintain a broad political consensus."[8] Yoshida and his successors followed a pragmatic course, determined to expand their power by creating a stable political and social order. As the urban middle class expanded during the period of high economic growth, the conservatives increasingly appealed to this constituency and its various new interest groups through successful economic policies and the provision of social services and social welfare. The conservatives thus broadened the social coalition supporting the LDP and coopted most of the issues on which the Socialists had staked their opposition.

Japan's Success and Progressive Decline. The progressives' radical critique of Japanese society, so popular in the early postwar period, lost its strength in the course of Japan's rapid economic growth and the consequent revival of confidence in Japanese abilities. In a thoughtful essay written in 1979, Komiya Ryūtarō drew attention to the rightward drift of opinion in the media. He estimated that until the mid-1960s 80 percent of opinion leaders were of the progressive persuasion, but this figure had been reversed and 80 percent were now of center or conservative leaning.[9]

Affluence undermined the appeal of the left wing. "The leftist intellectuals," observed an editorial writer for the *Nihon keizai shimbun* in 1979, "have not been able to cope with the sweeping changes that have occurred in the masses themselves over the past twenty years or so."[10] The traditional intellectual leadership had been replaced by "middle-class intellectuals": editorial writers, columnists in the media, bureaucrats, and businessmen, who lacked the depth and background of academic intellectuals but were more in tune with middle-class values. Surveys showed that 90 percent of the Japanese people regarded themselves as middle class. Progressives had failed to provide values consonant with the real conditions of economic growth. The middle-class intellectuals, however, addressed themselves to the tastes and interests of this broad new middle class. Above all, their writings dwelt on the Japanese character and traditions and fed the appetite for self-reflection and self-congratulation.

By the end of the 1970s, both in Japan and—more important for Japanese self-esteem—overseas it was readily acknowledged that Japan had advanced to the front rank as a global economic power. In the judgment of a chorus of contemporary observers, the nation had mastered the skills of organizing a modern industrial society with greater success than any other people, causing a Harvard sociologist to rate it simply number one in the world. However providential the international conditions had been for Japan's high-growth policies, the Japanese most often attributed their success to unique features in their own cultural environment. The Japanese began to regain trust in their own abilities. A succession of books by foreigners praising their achievements and analyzing the distinctiveness of their industrial organization started a trend toward cultural explanations of the Japanese success. The popular French writer Jean-Jacques Servan-Schreiber in his book *The World Challenge* (1981) asserted that "Japan stands as a model to all the world."

In the early postwar decades, when many Japanese had embraced the universalist pretensions of the new institutions established by the occupation, Japanese values and institutions were seen as somehow abnormal, distorted, unhealthy, and premodern. If Japan were to recover and develop into a modern, democratic, and progressive industrial society, it must eliminate these values and institutions and follow the path of the liberal-democratic nations of the West.

By the 1980s, however, in one of those ironies for which Clio is justly noted, history was turned on its head. Japan's traditional values—in some respects the very ones rejected after 1945 as a source of national weakness and shame—were now acclaimed not only by commentators in Japan but, perhaps even more important to the Japanese, by foreign observers as Japan's unique advantage

47

in building an advanced industrial society. No people can for long be satisfied to reject wholly the cultural heritage that is the legacy of their ancestors and the source of their *amour-propre*. Accordingly, given such economic success and acclaim for its cultural basis and the unmistakable signs that the stigma of the war years had been outlived and past sins atoned for, the Japanese mood changed.

For the progressives, the charge that the values and institutions they espoused were not products of Japan's own history and traditions was troublesome. Initially the progressive position rested on a highly critical evaluation of Japanese politics and society. As national self-confidence grew, the progressive position had less appeal, and progressives tried to reconcile the postwar system and its values with indigenous traditions.

Progressives tried to show, for example, that Article 9 was not foreign to Japanese traditions but rather had roots in the Japanese past. The prominent political scientist Maruyama Masao traced a strand of Japanese liberal thought that prepared the way for postwar pacifism. He found antecedents for Article 9 in the writings of such distinguished writers as Yokoi Shōnan, Ueki Emori, Kitamura Tōkoku, Uchimura Kanzō, Kinoshita Naoe, and Tokutomi Roka of the prewar era; he pointed to the platform of the Social Democratic party, which demanded in 1902 the abolition of armaments, and to the pronouncements of the *Heimin shimbun*, which opposed the Russo-Japanese War and advocated disarmament.[11]

Another leading political scientist, Kamishima Jirō, went farther back in Japanese history to find roots for pacifism and disarmament in Japanese tradition. Kamishima, who had never shared the critical stance of most progressives toward Japanese tradition, emphasized both Hideyoshi's sword hunt of 1588, which disarmed the civilian population, and the abolition of samurai swords in 1876, which left arms exclusively in the hands of the state. In this vein, he concluded that the Japanese people's determination to maintain Article 9 despite foreign pressure must be understood as "an extension of the tradition of disarmament in our country." He contrasted this tradition with the experience of Western countries, where modern revolutions required arming the common people to overthrow governments and led to recognition of the citizen's right to bear arms. Kamishima's effort to establish indigenous antecedents for postwar demilitarization seemed a bit forced in light of 600 years of feudal military tradition and of popular glorification of the *bushido* ethic in prewar Japan.[12]

In any case, it was one of the boldest efforts to meet criticism that the postwar order was alien to Japanese tradition.

Although frequently scorned as utopian pacifists whose views were divorced from the reality of power politics, progressives argued that military power was no longer the wave of the future and that national greatness would not be determined by such power. Their vision of the future, wrote Tsuru Shigeto, former Hitotsubashi economist and subsequently editorial advisor to the *Asahi shimbun*, was of a country "oriented toward respect for man." Japan should aspire to be a model of humanitarian ideals; it should strive to be known as the health care center of the world, a country of extraordinary scenic beauty to be visited by peoples from all over the globe, the leader in promotion of cultural exchange, the sponsor of the United Nations University, and the most generous contributor to developing countries and to refugee relief.[13]

Sakamoto Yoshikazu, professor of international politics at the University of Tokyo, set forth a vision of Japan's unique role in the modern world, stressing the following aspects of Japan's historical experience that would comprise a unique national identity as a model society:

1. As the only people to have suffered the effects of nuclear warfare, Japan had a mission to take the lead in opposing the spread of nuclear arms by stressing its three nuclear principles and working for a nuclear-free zone in Asia.

2. As the poorest in natural resources among the industrial nations, Japan could serve as an example of a highly efficient society, frugal in its use of the earth's resources.

3. As a country that suffered serious environmental crises during its industrialization, Japan could develop technology and legislation to minimize ecological destruction.

4. As a country that distinguished itself by its openness to foreign cultures, Japan could become a model of an open society by pursuing not only importation of culture but an open-door policy to refugees and immigration.

Sakamoto concluded, "There exist in Japan the distinctive elements of a national identity which could become the core of a new and universal model of society. The role of the Japanese people in the community of mankind should be to build on this foundation a nuclear-free, pollution-free, resource-saving, and open society."[14]

Economic Success and New Self-Confidence

The progressive vision of a transformed national character lost much of its appeal as economic success buoyed the national spirit. The surge of self-confidence was evidenced by the veritable tide of success literature that flooded the bookstores. Scores of books were written about the reasons for Japanese success; their common theme was an emphasis upon the unique characteristics of the Japanese people and their culture. Japan had outstripped the economic performance of other industrial countries, went the usual explanation, because its historically formed institutions had proved more productive and competitive than those of all other countries. More than one writer drew the irresistible conclusion. Wrote the widely read economist Iida Tsuneo, who subsequently toned down his remarks: "Is it not possible that Japan may be quite different from other countries? Is it not possible that Japan may be quite superior to other countries (*yohodo sugurete iru*)?"[15] A new national pride was palpable in the early 1980s. The November 17, 1984, *Asahi shimbun* reported that a majority of Japanese now regarded themselves as superior to Westerners. This conclusion was based on the 1983 *Survey of Japanese Character*, which the government conducts at five-year intervals. The *Asahi*, announcing the results of the 1983 survey, observed that one of the most striking changes of attitude over the thirty years since the first survey was the response to the question "Compared to Westerners, do you think, in a word, that the Japanese are superior? Or do you think they are inferior?" In 1953, 20 percent answered that the Japanese were superior. In 1983, 53 percent answered that the Japanese were superior.

These new attitudes toward the West developed as Japan's economic progress became apparent. As early as 1967, in an article entitled "Europe and Japan" by Umesao Tadao of Kyoto University, Europe was described as an object for sightseeing but no longer useful as a model. Umesao wrote of the "relative decline in status of the European countries in the postwar world" and held that "we are either moving shoulder to shoulder with Europe or are already out in front." He concluded that the "Japanese today cannot fail to perceive the bankruptcy of Europe."[16] By the late 1970s, Japanese periodicals widely discussed *Eikokubyō* (the British disease), which one writer in *Shokun* referred to as "a social disease which, upon the advancement of welfare programs, causes a diminished will to work, over-emphasis on rights, and declining productivity."[17]

Nor was the United States by any means exempt from such patronizing attitudes. After Vietnam, Watergate, and the seizure of American hostages in Iran, discussion of "America's fading glory" was not infrequent. An editorial writer, Matsuyama Yukio, for the *Asahi shimbun* wrote, "Watching the United States suddenly losing its magnificence is like watching a former lover's beauty wither away. It makes me want to cover my eyes."[18] Articles about the "American disease" also appeared, particularly in light of the conquest of the U.S. automobile industry. The American disease referred to a wasteful, inefficient society, bereft of its work ethic, no longer able to maintain the quality of its goods, crime- and divorce-ridden, suffering social disintegration. One Japanese journalist observed in December 1980 that there had formed

> an image in the Japanese mind of the United States as being hopeless. . . . Put sarcastically, the reason half a million copies of Ezra Vogel's *Japan as Number One* have been sold in Japan is that the book captures the psychology underlying the negative image of the United States and appeals to the Japanese sense of superiority.[19]

Conversely, in 1979 the director-general for foreign relations at the Defense Agency, Okazaki Hisahiko, cautioned his countrymen not to count out the Anglo-Saxons prematurely for they have "peculiar institutions that sometimes appear to be weak and on the verge of collapse. They have proved not to be weak, however, and those who have banked on their weakness have ended up losers." Okazaki concluded that "if we continue to bet on the Anglo-Saxons, we should be safe for at least twenty years."[20]

The Strength of Cultural Values. The cultural roots of Japanese success were emphasized not only at the popular level or only by foreign observers. An economic study group appointed by Prime Minister Ōhira in 1979 to advise him on management of the economy gave substantial credit to cultural factors in explaining its performance. Heavily representative of some of the country's best-known economists, the group in its report, published in 1980, traced the success of the economy to Japan's traditional cultural values:

> Unlike Western societies [which are based] on the "individual" or "self," the basic characteristic of Japanese culture is that, as shown in the Japanese word *ningen*, it values the "relationship between persons" (*hito to hito no aidagara*). In examining Japanese culture closely, we dis-

cover that this basic characteristic permeates, and acts as a living foundation for, the workings and the system of the Japanese economy. Rather than encouraging intense competition among individuals, with each being wholly responsible for his actions, the Japanese economy relies on "collegial groups" (*nakama shūdan*) that are based on various relationships created within and between companies. This tends to give rise to a phenomenon of dependence (*amae*) that is induced by mutual reliance (*motareai*) among persons. In some instances, such a relationship can be detrimental to "freedom" and "competition" and contains many undesirable aspects. However, the Japanese economy, which [as exemplified in the word] *ningen*, is the very model which Western societies are now beginning to emulate.[21]

The report found such interpersonal relationships fundamental to explaining the high motivation of workers and the continuing increases in productivity and exports realized by the economy:

Unlike the Western systems where each worker, isolated and insecure, must find meaning in life outside of his work, the intricately balanced combination of the long-term employment system and the seniority wage system in Japan provides Japanese workers with a sense of cohesion and security within this system of collegial groups. And these are the sources of the dynamic competition [among workers] for promotion and the vitality exhibited by the economic system as a whole. . . . These high-quality workers, providing vitality to their companies and improving company performance, are not like machinery or a handful of leaders; they cannot be imported from abroad. Because Japan has workers such as these, the superiority (*yūi-sei*) of the Japanese economy is unlikely to be lost in the near future.[22]

Similar group-oriented characteristics unique to Japanese culture accounted for the cohesion and the effective communication networks in the Japanese managerial system. The authors of the report then extended their analysis to inter-firm relationships and explained why competition among Japanese companies, also forming collegial groups of their own, was not detrimental to collective interest. The government played a positive, supporting role:

In Japan, along with buyers and sellers (in the market), the government too is a member of this collegial group [formed by government and industry], and the government does not have an adversary relationship with other participants in the market. Japan's administrative guidance (*gyōsei shidō*)—by now so internationally well-known that it is included in some English dictionaries—functions extremely efficiently. Westerners often ask the reasons for its success, and some of them, seeing it, use the phrase, "Japan, Inc."[23]

The assertion of the progressives that the monopolistic practices of Japanese business should be regulated were dismissed by the new conservative economists as ignorance of "the unique structure and ethics of Japanese society."[24] The economists argued that when the actual functioning of the Japanese economy was scrutinized, it would be seen to have more competition than Western economies because of the influence of certain Japanese cultural traits. The fierceness of competition, rather than the lack of competition, was the problem requiring regulation. The economist Iida wrote:

> I strongly feel that views such as "the Japanese economy is ridden with cartels, and oligopoly disease affects the core of the economy" and the like, which present Japan as the worst example of all, are results of intellectual laziness. . . . Much too much credence is given to the pet illusion of "progressive" intellectuals that if we "destroy" these "monopolies," all our problems will be solved.[25]

The belief of Iida and others'—that the Japanese economy had a degree of competition surpassing that of other industrial democracies—was one of the most interesting examples of the confidence of many Japanese that their economy behaved in a unique and superior fashion because of distinctive cultural patterns inherent in Japanese society.

The most colorful and creative spokesman of the argument of excessive competition (*katō kyōsō*) in Japan was Amaya, former MITI vice minister. In common with the economists' report to Prime Minister Ōhira, Amaya stressed the formation of collegial groups within the Japanese economy. These groups embraced a firm, its employees, other firms with which it did business, its subcontractors, and its bank. Holding these groups together was a sense of internal solidarity rooted in values of harmony that originated in the traditional village. Amaya held that these groups were therefore a combination of *Gesellschaft* and *Gemeinschaft* elements.

Such *Gemeinschaft*-like interpersonal relationships are not only between a firm and its employees. They also exist between one firm and others with which it has business relationships, and between a firm and its banks. These inter-firm relationships are not cold, profit-loss relationships based on calculations and contracts, but cohesive relationships which have a large margin for emotion and sense of obligation.[26]

Within the Japanese economy, Amaya contended, among these groups was an intense competition unknown in the West. Japanese struggles went far beyond the bounds of seeking only profit; they sought the prestige of larger market shares. Because of the collegial nature of relationships, employees were willing to sacrifice for their company, subcontractors would absorb losses, and banks would allow overborrowing to facilitate expansion. Antitrust regulation to preserve competition was necessary in Western societies because they did not have the cultural forces that promoted a fierce and excessive competition.

In Western societies where the first goal of firms is to make profits and where competition is only a means to achieve that goal, competition is waged only within bounds that assure them of profits. This is the first limit imposed on the severity of competition. If competition were to be waged beyond this limit, the dedication of the employees must be demanded in order to reduce the losses which the firm suffers from competition. But, in Western societies, such dedication cannot be expected of employees. This is the second limit imposed on the competition.

The basic principle behind the above limitations on competition is the principle of self-reliance. Even when management suffers from difficulties, it cannot rely on employees' sacrifices; it cannot press hard on subcontractors; and not much can be expected from the government or the banks in the way of assistance. All this acts as an effective brake on unconstrained competition.[27]

Amaya argued that Japanese society needed less to prevent combinations and monopolies than to regulate this destructive competition. Accordingly a national industrial policy and a regulating body like MITI were necessary to eliminate the dangers of ruinous internecine competition and to maintain order in the economy. Amaya observed that many groups in Japanese society—including the "so-called progressive-minded men of culture, those who believe that the Western pattern must be universal, a large number of journalists, and the progressive opposition parties"—failed to understand how history inevitably motivated Japanese employees to behave in ways different from their Western counterparts.[28]

The broad appeal of cultural explanations for Japanese success continued to draw strength during the 1980s from the mounting confidence of overtaking the West in technological capacity. A survey conducted by the Economic Planning Agency in 1985 found that among Japan's 1,600 leading firms 90 percent believed they had caught up with or surpassed the technological capacity of U.S. firms. By this time, most Japanese no longer believed that the nation should emulate foreign models. There was a pervasive belief that Japan had fulfilled the goal of the Meiji Restoration more than a century earlier of absorbing what the West had to offer.

More notable still, many Japanese writers began to argue that not only had Japanese culture allowed the nation to catch up in a material sense, but it had also led to the fulfillment of Western goals of individual freedom and equality in a more complete sense than had been achieved in the West. The views of the popular economic writer Iida Tsuneo can illustrate this attitude best:

> The nature of the Japanese economy is such that, in comparison to the United States and Europe, it better observes the spirit embodied in modern economics and more effectively functions in accordance with the principles of Neoclassical economic theory. In a broader perspective, one can say that the national characteristic of Japan, in comparison to the West, is to pursue more seriously such bourgeois democratic values as liberty, equality, and (respect for) the individual, and to realize these goals on a wider, more effective scale. In short, the basic character of Japan consists of purified strains (*junsui baiyō*) of the West.[29]

Out of the chrysalis of Japanese culture has come the purest expression of modern Western values. Japan's achievement was not simply a material one of outstripping the economic growth and per capita GNP of Western societies but a cultural one of actually fulfilling the most cherished aspirations of Western civilization. Iida wrote:

> Generally speaking, then, in terms of achieving the ideals of democracy, egalitarianism, and individualism and in

maintaining a competitive (economic) mechanism, Japan may appear to be an ordinary nation. But this "ordinariness" is only in appearance. The fact of the matter is that what are "principles" (*tatemae*) in the Western nations have become "reality" (*honne*) in Japan.[30]

In such a view, Japan's national character is more Western or modern than the prewar conception, which was fundamentally based on the formula of merging Western science and Japanese values. Iida concluded:

As is often said, Japan relies on the West for the principles of science and technology. But, in making improvements on, and in adapting [the imported science and technology], Japan often excels the West. Since this is the case with science and technology, there is nothing surprising about the fact that similar feats are being accomplished in the economic and social arenas.[31]

In short, the radical critique of Japanese institutions and values that had a wide appeal in the postwar decades was replaced in the 1980s by a prevalent belief that Japanese cultural values had the inherent capacity for transformation and adaptation to achieve universal goals of freedom and equality and that they were proving better suited to industrial society than their Western counterparts.

Political Nationalism and Opposition to the Yoshida Doctrine

Not surprisingly, this new-found confidence in the efficacy of Japanese abilities not only put the progressives on the defensive, it rekindled the political nationalism that had been repressed during the years of high economic growth in the 1960s and 1970s. When the Yoshida Doctrine was formulated in the 1950s, a group of conservatives and right-wing Socialists had opposed the strategy of exclusive preoccupation with economic nationalism and offered a different definition of Japanese purpose. They had advocated the restoration of Japan as a normal nation-state with its own independent military capacity and foreign policy. At the time of the Yoshida-Dulles negotiations, Ashida Hitoshi best exemplified this position. An exponent of cooperation with the Anglo-Saxon powers in the 1920s and an opponent of the militarism of the 1930s, he maintained his liberal stance through the dark days of the 1940s. In the postwar period, he championed the occupation and chaired the Constitution Review Committee in the

Diet, where, as discussed in chapter 2, he inserted amendments to Article 9 designed to allow self-defense and participation in UN peace-keeping forces. Ashida joined with conservative Socialists Katayama Tetsu and Nishio Suehiro in 1947–1948 to wrest control of the government briefly from Yoshida.

When the defense issue surfaced in 1950 with the outbreak of the Korean War, Ashida grew increasingly agitated. Several other conservatives as well as the right-wing Socialists could accept neither Yoshida's dependence on the U.S. security guarantee nor the left-wing Socialists' vision of an unarmed and neutral Japan. Ashida wrote in his diary one month after the war started: "I think the Japanese today are truly foolish and cowardly. There are fools who think the [Korean] incident is a war that concerns third parties with no relation to them."[32] He sought a middle way between Yoshida's cynical economics-first strategy and the neutralism of the Left. "It is impermissible," he wrote in December 1950, "for Japan alone to adopt the attitude of a bystander. Japan today is in urgent need of unifying its national purpose. . . . The government should explain to the people that Japan is on the brink of danger and that the Japanese people must resolve to defend the country by their own efforts."[33] In the January 20, 1951, declaration of the anti-Yoshida conservatives, known then as the Minshutō (the Democratic party), they asserted, "The Japanese are not a cowardly people who will rely on the occupation powers to preserve their stability and security while standing by with arms folded and without shedding a drop of blood."[34] Although Ashida voted for the peace and security treaties, he was critical of them as self-contradictory, on the one hand declaring an intention to share the burden of defense but on the other refusing to take positive steps to rearm.

While Yoshida pursued his strategy of resisting U.S. efforts to draw Japan into collective security arrangements in the Pacific, the opposition to this course among many conservatives was severe. These anti-Yoshida conservatives were motivated by a political nationalism that regarded an indefinite dependent status in security affairs as demeaning and who therefore favored revision of the constitution, rearmament, and an independent though pro-U.S. foreign policy. This independent policy gave pause to the U.S. leadership, which, while wishing rearmament, wanted a pliant, cooperative Japan.

This cause championed by Ashida was taken up by other politicians who had been purged and returned after the end of the occupation—most notably Hatoyama Ichirō and Kishi Nobusuke—as well as by young conservative mavericks like Nakasone Yasuhiro. They were able to join with the JSP and drive Yoshida from office at the end of 1954; for nearly six years they pursued their policies. Hatoyama and Kishi each embarked on a foreign policy initiative to demonstrate their commitment to a more independent stance backed by political nationalism. Hatoyama attempted to reach a peace treaty with the Soviet Union; Kishi sought to revise the security treaty with the United States to render it more equal. Both efforts ended in disarray and confusion. Hatoyama's attempt to settle the territorial dispute over the Northern Islands aborted; Kishi's renegotiation of the security treaty led to the greatest popular demonstrations in Japanese history. The Yoshida conservatives backed Kishi's treaty efforts only with the understanding that one of their own, Ikeda Hayato, would succeed him. When Ikeda took office, he immediately returned to the Yoshida strategy.

The success of the Yoshida Doctrine during the period of high growth suppressed political nationalism. Nevertheless the Yoshida strategy always had an Achilles' heel: the trade-off it made in terms of Japan's *amour-propre*. To depend on another country for its security and to suppress national pride was never easy, particularly for the conservatives, whose emotional attachment to nationalism was naturally strong. Their resentment was never far from the surface. In a frequently recounted incident, the conservative leader Shiina Etsusaburō in Diet proceedings once referred to the Americans as "the watchdogs at the gate (*banken*)" protecting Japan. When another Diet member questioned whether it was rude and insulting to call the Americans "dogs," Shiina in mock apology responded, "Excuse me. They are honorable watchdogs at the gate (*banken-sama*)."[35] The leading theorist of the conservative establishment, Kōsaka Masataka, frequently admitted that the greatest challenge of the Yoshida strategy was how to maintain national morale.

Rebirth of Political Nationalism. Political nationalism was quiescent in the two decades after the massive 1960 riots over the security treaty, but inevitably the immense pride in Japan's economic achievement led to its resurgence in the 1980s. Many high-profile media figures such as Ishihara Shintarō, Etō Jun, and Shimizu Ikutarō, appealing to this new pride, argued that Japan should acquire military power commensurate with its new economic strength and should exercise an independent political role in the world. They mounted an assault on the postwar system, the constitution and other American-sponsored reforms, and the Yoshida strategy as responsible for the nation's lack of political vitality and will.

Intent on discrediting the constitution, many political nationalists, of whom the writer Etō Jun was the most notable, scrutinized the procedures followed in drafting and imposing the constitution. They emphasized the censorship, the manipulation of popular opinion, and the alien and utopian nature of its provisions. The resulting constitutional system deprived Japan of sovereign rights fundamental to a nation-state. "The basic goal of U.S. occupation policy," wrote Etō, "was to destroy the greater Japanese empire, which had styled itself as 'unparalleled among nations [bankoku muhi],' and to create an ordinary Japan. Ironically, the Occupation gave birth to a Japan that is, in an entirely different sense, 'unparalleled among nations.'" Without the "right of belligerency," which was renounced in Article 9, Japan could not be a free, sovereign nation, "master of its own fate."[36] Yoshida accepted this servile status and built Japan's postwar system to suit it. For Etō, "so long as we continue to set up Yoshida politics as the legitimate conservative politics, we Japanese will not escape from the shackles of the postwar period, and the road to self-recovery will be closed."[37] Since the administration of Prime Minister Ikeda, Etō believed, the government had shelved the constitutional issue, concentrated on economic development, and interpreted the constitution to suit the government's needs as they arose. Etō maintained that a tacit understanding existed between the conservatives and progressives to leave the constitutional issue unresolved.

But the time had come, he wrote in 1980, to confront the issue and to restore Japan's right of belligerency so that the nation could prepare to defend itself should the need arise. Americans for their part must also face up to the new situation of Japanese power. They must admit that Article 9 was the result of their distrust of Japan and their fear that Japan might someday again attack the United States. "If there were among the American people the determination to wipe away completely their distrust of Japan, to tolerate a more powerful and less dependent Japan and to form an alliance with and coexist with such a Japan, the future of Japan-U.S. relations would be bright."[38]

The political nationalists argued that the renunciation of military power distorted national life. By relinquishing military strength, wrote the sociologist Shimizu Ikutarō, Japan ceased to be a state and instead became simply a society whose essence was economic activity. Katsuda Kichitarō, a professor of political thought at Kyoto University, observed in his book *Heiwa kempō o utagau* (Doubts about the peace constitution) that the postwar liberal constitutional order, in reaction to wartime nationalism, lost sight of the concept of the state to which citizens owe their loyalty so that it can maintain order and protect the welfare of the whole community. Instead, he wrote, business firms could call on their employees for the ultimate sacrifice. When a director of Nisshō-Iwai was implicated in a scandal involving the Grumman Corporation, he took his own life, leaving behind a note: "The company is eternal. Employees must die for the company."[39] As an illustration of the disgraceful weakness of the postwar state, Katsuda and other critics cited the hijacking of a Japan Airlines jet in 1977 by the radical group known as the Japanese Red Army. The government wholly capitulated, paying the $6 million ransom, releasing several terrorists from jail as demanded by the hijackers, and justifying its action by proclaiming that "a single human life is weightier than the earth."[40]

Setting the political nationalists apart was their belief that Japan should exercise an independent role in world politics. Shimizu Ikutarō, undoubtedly the nationalist writer attracting the most attention in the early 1980s, wrote in his sensational book *Nippon yo, kokka tare* (Japan, become a state!), published in 1980, "On the one hand Japan must encourage friendly relations with the United States, the Soviet Union, and all other countries, but at the same time we must not forget for an instant that Japan is alone. In the end we can only rely on Japan and the Japanese."[41] Shimizu was one of the most conspicuous critics of the postwar order and its values because he himself was a convert from the progressive camp. Observing the decline in U.S. power and world commitment, he came to believe that Japan must possess an independent deterrent capability. As a consequence, he and other political nationalists sought more than a modest buildup of arms. "If Japan acquired military power commensurate with its economic power," wrote Shimizu, "countries that fully appreciate the meaning of military power would not overlook this. They would defer; they would act with caution; and in time they would show respect." The time had arrived to fulfill Japan's potential:

> When Japan breaks down its postwar illusions and taboos and develops military power commensurate with its economic strength, significant political power will naturally be born. In its relations with the United States, the Soviet

Union, and many countries in many degrees and meanings, Japan will gain a free hand. Even though it be alone, if it exercises its political power wisely Japan will gain friends that will respect it and that will readily come to its aid. With its combined economic, military, and political power, won't Japan be a proud superpower (*dōdō taru tai-koku*)! While splendidly possessing the qualities to be a superpower, Japan, whether out of inertia or lack of courage, is behaving like a physically handicapped person right in plain view of the world.[42]

Pressing on relentlessly to his most dramatic point, Shimizu observed that the nuclear powers,

even though they do not use their weapons, are able to instill fears in those countries that do not have them. A country like Japan that does not possess nuclear weapons and is afraid of them will be easy game for the nuclear powers. Putting political pressure on Japan would be like twisting a baby's arm.[43]

Japan, in short, must "exercise the nuclear option."

The political nationalists reveled in the strategic debates that their views provoked in the 1980s. They confronted directly and insistently the contradictions and incongruities that characterized Japan's postwar order, and they advocated clear and decisive resolutions that touched deep and ambivalent emotions among many Japanese. Japan, Shimizu wrote, is a "peculiar" and "abnormal" country (*ijō na kuni*).[44] It had lived for decades under a constitutiional order forced on it by occupying military forces. It had abnegated the essential characteristics of a nation-state: military power and the required loyalty of its citizens. Other nations had lost a war, but had any other wholly lost its national consciousness?[45]

The dual uses of technology gave the nationalists confidence that Japan could play an independent role in international politics. In his 1987 book, *The Japanese-American War Is Not Finished* (*Nichi-bei sensō wa owatte inai*), Etō Jun exhorted his countrymen not to lose to the Americans in the high-tech rivalry, for technology could become the ultimate instrument of Japanese recovery from World War II. In a typical passage he wrote:

Actually the electronic technology capability presently being developed by Japan could be combined with rocket technology so that we could independently send up satellites and obtain accurate information as to the whereabouts of nuclear submarines. . . . Japan could announce its knowledge to the world. . . . Knowing the movement not only of Soviet but also of American nuclear submarines means that Japan would gain bargaining strength and could intermediate between the U.S. and the Soviet Union. . . . Japan will greatly raise her autonomous and central strategic position in the world. And accordingly Japan's international political voice will rise dramatically.[46]

In his cowritten tract *The Japan That Can Say No* (1989) Ishihara Shintarō conveyed the same message. Their prowess in technology will allow the Japanese to shake loose from their dependence and deference toward Americans. The latter will be compelled to recognize that "a new type of Japanese is coming on the scene. Japan's new technology is bringing the new Japanese into being." As they realize that the Americans will be increasingly dependent on their more advanced semiconductors and electronic equipment, the Japanese will grow more self-confident and assertive in international politics:

It should come as a pleasure for us Japanese, who alone have experienced the tragedy of a nuclear holocaust and who have pledged never to use nuclear weapons, to find that we are attaining a position where we can render the superpowers' nuclear warheads harmless by holding back the semiconductors they depend on. What could be a more fitting revenge for Hiroshima?[47]

Differences between 1930s and 1980s. Although the extremism, emotionalism, and anti-Americanism of the political nationalism that revived in the 1980s, and persists in the 1990s, are sometimes reminiscent of the ultranationalism of the 1930s, there are fundamental differences. Ultranationalism reflected that time. Circumstances in Japan and in the world are not the same as then. Fears of a revival of the nationalist movements of the prewar period are unwarranted for several reasons. First, prewar nationalism was fueled by the intense drive to catch up with the West, triggering intense feelings of inferiority, insecurity, and resentment toward the West. Japan's current self-confidence and pride in its achievements are not the same as the earlier ultranationalism, which was generated to compensate for its backwardness. That ultranationalism became virulent and pathological as the country struggled to overcome the West's more advanced economic and technological development.

Second, the elite leadership of the 1930s and the 1980s had starkly contrasting roles. The prewar elites mobilized and manipulated nationalism to justify their own position and to inspire the massive effort required of the Japanese people in the quest for industrial and imperial greatness. Japan's government today shows limited evidence of attempts to stimulate any similarly narrow political nationalism. Despite controversy over them in the 1980s, the wording of high school textbooks and official visits to Yasukuni Shrine are of a different nature from the intense bureaucratic campaigns of the prewar period designed to activate national loyalties and to subdue domestic unrest and tension. Today the elites more often seek to contain, if not to suppress, political nationalism. The mainstream adherents of the Yoshida Doctrine find it in Japan's national interest to pursue economic development and technological achievement. For them, the rise of political nationalism could portend their loss of mastery over Japanese political developments. The cautious and shrewd pursuit of Japanese interests in the postwar period has depended upon a pragmatic approach that would be greatly complicated by popular nationalism. Moreover, it could greatly complicate Japan's foreign relations and potentially jeopardize its international economic interests by creating suspicions and fear of Japanese intentions. For all these reasons, the mainstream elites on the whole seek to preserve the Yoshida strategy. They are beginning to encourage internationalization in a variety of ways because this, in contrast to a narrow political nationalism, is more often seen in Japan's interest.

Third, prewar nationalism drew on symbols of the traditional culture. The native folk religion was politicized, while the bureaucracy used the emperor as its supreme symbol to inspire a people emerging from the isolation of feudalism. Today the older generation is attached to symbols of prewar nationalism, but indifference is the rule with the postwar generation. As Murakami Yasusuke, who has studied contemporary middle-class society, described the situation: "Public opinion polls indicate that the new middle mass has little motivation for recreating a Japanese identity centered around any traditional symbol. This is especially true of the younger generation, whose growing indifference to the Emperor is conspicuous."[48] Popular reaction to the death of Emperor Shōwa and the accession of the new emperor strongly confirm these views. Nationalist and right-wing movements do adhere to the traditional nationalist symbols, but these movements have had little success and then only when they moderate their means and ends.

Fourth, prewar nationalism was rooted in the lower middle class and in the villages with their resentment of urban values. The bearers of nationalism were the shopkeepers, small business-men, elementary school principals, and government and business clerical workers who had risen only partway up the educational ladder of success and who resented industrialism and the luxury and corruption of big business and party politicians. But Japan has seen the transformation of its social structure. Reflecting the values and tastes of affluence and industrialism, postwar Japan is overwhelmingly middle class and urban; its well-educated and well-read people are likewise well traveled and in some ways perhaps as well informed of world affairs as any people.

Fifth, Japan is rapidly increasing its interaction with other countries, unlike its seclusion from them in the 1930s. Internation-alization, despite its many uncertainties, is nonetheless the goal promoted at many levels of society. Nationalism is still the most powerful political emotion, however, and Japan is not immune to it. But the pervasive nationalist mood in today's Japan emanates principally from pride and self-assurance gained from achieving the national goal since World War II: catching up with the West. Global and country-specific circumstances are leading to a differ-ent kind of nationalism than what prevailed in the 1930s.

5

A New Definition
of National Interest

The efflorescence of political nationalism during the 1980s in the bombast of Shimizu Ikutarō, Ishihara Shintarō, Etō Jun, Nakagawa Yatsuhiro, and other extravagant media figures made lively copy. It titillated the self-satisfaction of the reading public and the sensationalism of editors and publishers. In 1990, when the U.S. public was given a whiff of this heady pride in the translation of Morita Akio's and Ishihara's *The Japan That Can Say No*, it led to expressions of outrage at Japanese arrogance and of concern that Japan might again be entering a period of ultranationalism.

But we ought not to mistake this political nationalism in the 1980s with a nationalist movement in any organized sense. It is rather a formless breast-beating pride in the postwar accomplishment mixed with more than a little frustration over the continuing subordination of Japan's political will in international affairs to the United States. However great the appeal of such fulminations to the Japanese *amour-propre*, the Japanese elites understand that Japan's self-interest does not lie down this path.

On the contrary, confident that Japan had at last caught up with the Western industrial economies, some of the political, business, and bureaucratic leaders were beginning to grope in the 1980s for a broader conception of Japanese national interest than that represented by the Yoshida strategy or the resurgent political nationalism. I have sometimes referred to this incipient new world view as Japan's new internationalism in that political and business leaders began to envision an active leadership role in international affairs, cooperating with the other industrial nations to support the international order in which they felt a growing stake. In this sense, they were internationalists. But this term is easily misunderstood. There was no Wilsonianism in this view. These internationalists were every bit as intent on pursuit of the Japanese national interest as the political nationalists, but they began to define this interest in broader terms because of changed conditions in the international system and particularly because of Japan's rapid rise in the system. One knowledgeable observer accordingly termed their views "internationalist nationalism" (*kokusaiteki nashonarizumu*).[1]

At the beginning of the 1980s, Japan's growing trade surplus had become a mounting challenge for the stability of the international system. Japanese were shocked that the French foreign trade minister had remarked in 1981 that "if Japan and the Soviet Union were to disappear from the face of the earth, we could live happily."[2] The U.S. business economist James Abegglen, ordinarily a defender of Japan's international position, wrote in 1980, "All of Japan's interactions with the rest of the world in trade, investment, aid, and defense, can be interpreted as those of a country acting purely in self-interest, with regard only to consequences for itself," and he criticized Japan for selfishly "refusing to undertake initiatives in international policy."[3] More than any other major economy, Japan was dependent on other nations. For the foreseeable future, it would need ever-increasing supplies of materials, foodstuffs, and fuels. Likewise, it needed a healthy world trade system, an open international economy, and a stable secure world order to guarantee access to materials and markets. Yet in amassing trade surpluses, administering niggardly and self-serving overseas aid and investment programs, and shunning all strategic affairs, it was pursuing a narrow self-interest, which drew increasing foreign hostility in the early 1980s. Denis Healey, former British chancellor of the Exchequer, complained at the time:

> For two years now, I have served as Chairman of the Interim Committee of the International Monetary Fund, but I have never seen Japan speak up before others do. Even when Japan did, it was simply in support of a majority opinion. Japan should play a more positive part in regard to the international monetary and economic problems.[4]

Ironically, the Yoshida Doctrine, which was partly intended to restore Japan's international reputation by projecting a peaceful image, ultimately demeaned Japan's stature. Consciously avoiding international controversy, maintaining a low posture, and limiting its public statements to platitudes, Japan cut almost no image on the world stage, where its political leaders were of little stature. The Japanese decision-making process always had tended to inhibit a bold, personalized style of leadership; the postwar desire to avoid political positions accentuated this tendency. Moreover, the infrequent debates on strategic issues were dominated by domestic concerns and divorced from the realities of international power politics. A former Japanese diplomat, Itō Kenichi, repelled by what he called a tradition of "my home diplomacy," recalled in 1980 the faceless procession of Japanese politicians coming through the Washington embassy, where he had served, wanting their pictures taken with prominent senators but having nothing of substance or significance to discuss with them. Itō, who subsequently formed a prominent Japanese foreign policy institute, argued that political obligations inevitably accompany vast economic power and that Japan could not continue to sit on the sidelines of global and regional strategic affairs with no clear foreign policy other than dependence on the United States and maintenance of good relations with all countries.[5]

Beginning in the late 1970s, significant numbers of the Japanese political, bureaucratic, and business elites expressed the view that Japan's own interests would no longer be served by pursuit of mercantilist policies and passive adjustment to prevailing international conditions. This new world view expounded by some of Japan's most prominent leaders rested on the belief that so great was Japan's stake in the international political-economic order, because of its export of goods and capital, that now, more than ever in the past, to be a Japanese nationalist was to be an internationalist. There were three fundamental tenets of this new internationalism:

1. It is in Japan's national interest to give support and leadership to the institutions of a liberal international economic order.

2. Japan must of its own initiative and to its own advantage reform its institutions to bring them into harmony with international norms and expectations.

3. The Japanese must develop a global consciousness and a liberal nationalism that while taking pride in their own heritage is open to and tolerant of other nationalities and cultures based upon a broad conception of national interest that acknowledges Japan's growing interdependency with the rest of the world.

On the face of it, the notion of a genuine Japanese internationalism must evoke skepticism. It appears almost oxymoronic, for nothing stirs greater exasperation from foreign observers of Japan, even those who have devoted their careers to understanding Japanese culture, than Japanese parochialism. The literary critic Edward Seidensticker wrote in his last column for the *Yomiuri* in 1962, "[The Japanese] are not like other people. They are infinitely more clannish, insular, parochial, and one owes it to one's self-respect to preserve a feeling of outrage at the insularity."[6] Edwin Reischauer, former ambassador to Japan and probably the leading foreign interpreter of Japanese civilization, was of the same mind. He wrote in 1978, "[The Japanese] must overcome their sense of separateness and, to put it bluntly, show a greater readiness to join the human race."[7] Dan F. Henderson, galled by the persisting legal restrictions of this "quasi-state-trading-regime," characterized Japan in 1986 as "a homogeneous insular enclave" whose liberal rhetoric was little more than an "insular internationalism."[8] Shortly before his death, Reischauer wrote in 1990 that Japan had become a "money-bloated giant" that had "earned itself a reputation for being a thoroughly egocentric country interested only in its own welfare, and yet its continued well-being or even existence depends on international cooperation and trust."[9]

The weight of Japanese history and culture is undoubtedly on the side of a deeply ingrained and persistent ethnocentrism. The social, cultural, and historical barriers to the Japanese achievement of a broader conception of their national interest are truly formidable. Nevertheless, we need to examine the effort of Japanese elite leadership to shape a different kind of national consensus of Japanese purpose because it represents their first attempt to adjust to changes in the international environment and to the new era that Japan confronts in coming to terms with its new power.

Ōhira and the New Intellectual Ferment

The cabinet of Prime Minister Ōhira Masayoshi (1978–1980) began the effort to define a new purpose for Japan's recently acquired economic power. Ōhira appointed a series of blue-ribbon commissions to debate and to formulate a national agenda for Japan as it approached the twenty-first century. An essential part of the task was to formulate a vision of the society that technology was likely to create. During its catch-up struggle, Japan always had an image of its future. But now increasingly it was a pioneer seeking to chart the future course of economic, technological, and social organization.

The Ōhira administration took office at the end of the 1970s at a heady time for Japan in view of the international attention its achievements were attracting. He himself had exulted in 1975:

> I think that from a world perspective, the Japanese are an extraordinarily excellent people (*hijō ni sugureta minzoku*). Through their long history, they have endured many trials and overcome many perils. Despite defeat they did not lose heart, but built today's state and society. . . . Poor in natural resources, our country's greatest resource is the Japanese people (*minzoku*).[10]

Ōhira believed that Japan had come to the end of the catch-up era and that the Liberal Democratic party (LDP) needed to modernize its thinking and to adopt new policies for a new era. Reflective and bookish by nature, an active Christian in his younger days, Ōhira called into being a remarkable intellectual effort to define a purpose for Japan's newly acquired economic power. Shortly after he was elected prime minister, he asked a bureaucratic aide, Nagatomi Yūichirō, to assemble prominent intellectuals and bureaucrats to assess the likely direction of change in the two decades leading up to the twenty-first century and to recommend policies that the LDP should pursue. He declared in his first address to the Diet as prime minister on January 25, 1979:

> For over thirty years since the war, we have striven singlemindedly with remarkable success in pursuit of economic affluence. This was the culmination of the more than 100 years of modernization patterned after Western models since the Meiji Restoration. . . . We are, if you will, on the threshold of a new age transcending the age of modernization (*kindai o koeru jidai*) and moving from an age centered on the economy to an age stressing culture.[11]

Ōhira's experience had been closely associated with the Ministry of Finance, and he was widely regarded as part of the LDP mainstream with its attachment to the Yoshida strategy. In sum, although his own thinking often seemed vague and visionary, Ōhira sensed that the policies pursued to achieve high economic growth had outlived their usefulness and that a change of course was needed. In one of his last addresses to the Diet, in January 1980, Ōhira was groping for a new policy agenda for the LDP:

The conditions which supported this rapid economic growth exist no longer. . . . Circumstances demand that we alter our industrial structure and way of life. . . . The problem confronting mankind today is that of how to sustain modernization's successes achieved thus far and how to develop them into the twenty-first century.[12]

After World War II, most of the intellectual community had been alienated from the political establishment. But the economic success of Japan, the stagnation of progressive politics, the pragmatism and welfare reforms of the LDP, generational change, and the attractions of proximity to political power, all helped to overcome this alienation during the 1970s. Ōhira's staff, with Nagatomi's energetic leadership, succeeded in assembling 130 of the country's leading intellectuals, together with eighty-nine leading bureaucrats, and divided them into nine research groups to debate and to formulate a national agenda for Japan as it approached the twenty-first century. Membership in the research groups included a substantial number of scientists and economists. Left-wing progressive intellectuals were passed over. Bureaucratic members were vice ministers, directors of bureaus, and others likely to be of long-range influence in the civil service. Aside from the more senior leaders of the study groups, most members had graduated from the universities between 1955 and 1965 and were therefore still relatively young.[13]

The nine research groups were each to study and to formulate policies on different subjects relating to Japan's future: culture, urban living, family life, life style, science and technology, macroeconomic management, economic foreign policy, pan-Pacific solidarity, and comprehensive national security. Meeting with the members of the research groups, Ōhira gave them their charge:

Our country has reached the first rank in science and technology and can no longer rely on the importation of science and technology from the advanced Western countries. The Japanese are a people that from ancient times have abounded with creative spirit. The fact that in the process of modernization we could quickly absorb Western science and technology and make it our own was the result of our country's own store of scientific and technological talent. From here on, we must develop Japan's own science and technology. I hope you will study these matters by adopting a long time-horizon and a broad perspective. For this purpose we have assembled not only professors of natural sciences but people from every field. I hope you will debate these matters freely and make your proposals to me.[14]

The research groups met for a year and a half, but Ōhira lived to read only three of the reports. He died in office in June 1980 and was briefly succeeded by the Suzuki administration (1980–1982). The work of the research groups continued after Ōhira's death. Nakasone was the first prime minister to read all nine reports. Shortly after taking office in November 1982, Nakasone met with the groups and told them that his agenda would be heavily influenced by the results of their research.[15]

A related and even more extensive intellectual effort was organized in 1984 to follow up on many of the recommendations from the Ōhira study groups. This time the Ministry of Finance brought together seventy scholars and 400 younger researchers from universities, ministries, and businesses to study the structural transformation of Japanese society and economy. Divided into thirty-nine research teams, they studied themes relating to the new technology and its implications for domestic and international change in the twenty-first century.[16]

A Neoconservative Agenda

Out of this extraordinary mobilization of intellectuals, bureaucrats, and business leaders came a neoconservative agenda for the 1980s. The term "neoconservatism" referred in part to the goal of replacing the conservatism of the late developer—the policies and consensus on catch-up modernization—that had guided Japanese domestic and foreign policies in the postwar decades. The term also referred to the many common themes shared with the Reagan and Thatcher neoconservative movements, which were ascendant at the same time.[17]

Neoconservatism in Japan shared many characteristics superficially with Reaganomics and Thatcherism. All emphasized small government, deregulation, greater reliance on market forces, and a more strident confrontation with the Soviet bloc. Japanese neoconservatism, however, differed markedly from its analogues in the United States and England in that it came at the end of a century-long, national campaign to overtake those same industrial nations. During this campaign, government had mobilized all the resources of the nation for a " 'total war' called high economic growth."[18] The Ōhira Research Groups argued that having achieved the purpose for which it was built, the structure of government controls needed to be relaxed. By the 1970s readily borrowable technology had been largely exhausted. In most fields, Japan had reached the frontier. The case for bureaucratic guidance was persuasive when Japan was still behind and the industrial future was clear, but its effectiveness was not so easily demonstrable when Japan had caught up. Moreover, as the most insightful studies have shown, administrative guidance consisted of policies that were mutually evolved by business and government. By the 1970s business was increasingly seeking a relaxation of controls that would permit it greater freedom and flexibility. Neoconservatism in England and the United States was a reaction to the policies of the welfare state, but in Japan it meant a departure from the regulations of catch-up economic growth.

At the outset of his prime ministership, in a statement of his views, which he later said drew on the Ōhira Research Groups, Nakasone explained why Japan needed administrative reform:

> During the process of modernization, when Japan was busily trying to catch up with the advanced nations of the West, the role of administration was to guide, supervise, and control. Now that Japan has caught up, this role has become unnecessary—or rather it has become in some ways a hindrance to the free activities of the private sector. Any further continuation of a pattern of dependence whereby the government's duty is indulgently presumed to be the provision of services for the nation will mean a waste of funds. The time has come for a compact "small government" concerned with shaping policies and legislation that will serve as guideposts.[19]

The Ōhira Research Groups recommended the establishment of an "administrative reorganization office" in the cabinet with a three-year plan to streamline government and to make it more open.[20] Japanese neoconservatives believed that the machinery of government built up over the century of modernization could lead Japan to develop its own strain of "advanced countries' disease" (senshinkoku byō). One influential adviser to Ōhira and subsequently to Nakasone of this mind was Kōyama Ken'ichi, founder of Group 1984, a conservative organization that was established after the first oil shock and was preoccupied with the excesses of government. Kōyama, who during his student days had been a leader of the radical Zengakuren but whose thinking had subsequently changed, and Group 1984 authored a series of influential books. Eikoku-byō no kyōkun (The lessons of the British disease) and Nihon no jisatsu (The suicide of Japan) were both directed at the proliferation of bureaucracy and the need for institutional reform. *Gendai no majokari* (Witch hunting in modern times) was an attack on investigations of environmental pollution. These books were popular with business groups. The chairman of Keidanren (Federation of Economic Organizations), Dokō Toshio, in particular was taken by *The Suicide of Japan*, published in 1976, and personally sponsored the reprinting of 100,000 copies of a portion of the book. Many parallel developments gave rise to the movement for small government: the end of the high-growth period after the oil shock, the growing government debt because of new welfare commitments, the expansionary fiscal policy of the Fukuda administration in response to its "international pledge" to play the role of a locomotive economy, public opposition to Ōhira's proposed tax increase, and the emergence of Reaganomics and the like-minded philosophy of Prime Minister Thatcher.

Nakasone shrewdly grasped these trends and had himself appointed to Suzuki Zenkō's cabinet as the minister in charge of the Administrative Management Agency. In this position, he prevailed on Suzuki in the fall of 1980 to form a commission for administrative reform (*Rinchō*) under Nakasone's leadership. Dokō, revered in the business community for his integrity and Spartan life style, assumed the chairmanship of the commission. Although it was an official commission and its membership had to have some semblance of balance, Nakasone found ways to pack it with neoconservatives, many from the Ōhira Research Groups. Besides serving as a vehicle for Nakasone's ascent to power when the hapless Suzuki faltered in 1982, it also became the opening wedge in the neoconservative effort to reduce the role of government.

Neoconservatism not only saw the end of the long catch-up phase in Japanese history, it proclaimed the opening of a new one in which the Japanese would be more reliant on their own cultural resources to determine national progress. The Ōhira Research Group on the Age of Culture emphasized the juncture that had been reached. For more than a century, Japan had denigrated its own heritage by acknowledging the superiority of Western culture. In its single-minded pursuit of industrial civilization, Japan had largely ignored the development of its own heritage to import Western practical knowledge. But the success in overtaking the West and in producing superior manufactures had led to a worldwide interest in Japanese culture. "Japanese culture is no longer simply the possession of the Japanese."[21] In this new age of culture, as Ōhira had perceived it, the Japanese would not only

73

return to their own cultural values but would also share these values with a universal audience. As Japan had adopted nearly all the available technology, there was a belief that a new wave of technological innovation was beginning and the Japanese were positioned to become its leaders.

These neoconservative views on domestic policy issues were inextricably tied to neoconservative foreign policy views, for the end of catch-up inevitably implied a reassessment of foreign policy. The Ōhira Research Group on Comprehensive Security declared that a new era in international relations was beginning: "The most fundamental change in the international situation that took place in the 1970s is the termination of clear American supremacy in both military and economic spheres." The Soviet military buildup and the economic development of Japan and Europe had changed the system. "As a result, it has become impossible to rely primarily upon the United States as in the past for the maintenance of the international currency system and the free trade system." The Yoshida Doctrine, therefore, had to be reassessed: "It has become impossible for Japan to pursue solely its own economic interests within this system."[22] In sum, the neoconservative espousal of a new internationalism began in the recognition of the end of Japanese catch-up modernization and the assertion of the end of Pax Americana.

Internationalization and Internationalism

It is useful to distinguish between internationalization and internationalism. The former, as used here, refers to the process of liberalization by which Japanese policies and institutions are harmonized with international practice. Internationalization as a process has been dependent on foreign pressure to provide the impetus for liberalization of the Japanese political economy. Internationalism, conversely, is a set of political beliefs arguing that internationalization is in Japan's best interests and that Japan should therefore on its own initiative and without outside prodding pursue the process.

Internationalization of Japanese trade practices, of the Japanese financial system, and of Japanese capital flows began in the mid-1960s. Once Japan joined the Organization of Economic Cooperation and Development (OECD) in 1964, the nation was, in Chalmers Johnson's words, "committed not only to trade liberalization but also to the removal of controls on capital transactions. The 'fully opened economy' was at last on the nation's agenda."[23]

Nevertheless, resistance to liberalization was fierce both in the business community and in the bureaucracy. Fear of isolation in the world community and the exercise of foreign pressure set liberalization in motion and kept it going. Komiya Ryūtarō and Itoh Motoshige recall that it was likened to the arrival of Commodore Perry's black ships in 1853, which compelled the opening of Japanese ports to foreign trade. Joining international organizations like GATT, OECD, and the IMF was necessary to secure export markets around the world. The obligations of internationalization that accompanied admission to these organizations were, however, thought dangerous by Japanese leaders: "Liberalization of imports, inward direct investments, and foreign exchange controls were thought of as a 'necessary cost' or a 'sacrifice' that Japan had to pay in order to secure membership in the international club of major industrialized countries."[24]

As a consequence of this negative attitude, the process moved slowly—and largely in relation to the degree of foreign presure that was exerted. In MITI an "international faction" came to the forefront of leadership at the beginning of the 1970s and facilitated the process of internationalization not because it was a positive good but rather because it was inevitable. As Chalmers Johnson describes this faction: "Most of them had served overseas, were well versed in the 'culture' of international commerce (which involved institutions such as the IMF, GATT, and the OECD, and trends such as capital liberalization). . . . They are accurately described as 'cosmopolitan nationalists.' "[25] They were mercantilists, still intent on preserving the ministry's role in support of catch-up policies, while recognizing that accommodation to foreign demands was necessary. Amaya Naohiro, who became vice minister for international affairs in 1980, was a good example of this international faction; his essay expounding the merchant nation thesis was discussed in chapter 3. A "major sign of internationalization" in Johnson's view was the revision of the Foreign Exchange and Foreign Trade Control Law of 1949 (FECL) and the abolition of the Foreign Capital Law of 1950. These changes, effective in 1980, dismantled MITI's main statutory powers, in Johnson's judgment. Henderson, however, maintains that "the basic restrictive potential of the old FECL remains . . . Liberal in spirit the law is not."[26]

However one interprets the tangled and multifaceted process of internationalization, which is too complex a topic to treat here, observers agree that it has been a slow process and dependent on foreign pressure to succeed. Even Komiya and Itoh, who present a perspective decidedly sympathetic to Japanese policies, agree that "it took a long time, therefore, for trade liberalization, capital liberalization, and liberalization of foreign exchange controls to be nearly completed or to finish the first stage. . . . The pace of liberalization was much influenced by the strength of external pressure for liberalization."[27]

Political Beliefs and the New Internationalism

Let us now turn from the process of internationalization to the political beliefs underlying the new internationalism. Where the process of internationalization had been driven by negative attitudes, prodded by foreign demands and the fear of isolation, the internationalism of the neoconservatives was impelled by self-confident views of the value of accommodating the international system. Because neoconservatives saw internationalization in Japan's self-interest, they held positive attitudes toward the process and sought to take the initiative rather than to wait for foreign pressure. They were less fearful than they were appalled at the prospects of isolation. They were impatient with bureaucratic resistance and believed that continued pursuit of narrow mercantilist policies would not only isolate Japan, it would undermine the liberal international order upon which Japan depended. They understood better than most bureaucrats that Japanese policies were seen as a challenge to the international system.

As the structure of Japan's economy changed, particularly after the first oil crisis in 1973–1974, as Japan emerged as the second largest free-market economy in the world, and as its share in world trade, especially export of manufactures, grew conspicuously large, some Japanese leaders realized that Japanese prosperity was increasingly dependent on the existence of a healthy, open, free trade order. And as U.S. commitment to a liberal international political economy showed signs of wavering, these leaders' appreciation of its benefits grew.

Fundamentally this realization was a matter of the dramatic improvements in Japan's industrial capability and its comparative advantage. In the early postwar decades, Japan's comparative advantage was in labor-intensive products that were dependent on cheap but high quality labor. Over time, the economy was able to move ahead under the aegis of the high-growth system; by the late 1970s, "the pattern of Japan's comparative advantage shifted toward processing and assembling-type manufacturing industries that depend on mass-production methods and medium to high technologies." As the industries in which Japan had a comparative advantage moved up the product cycle and as these products gained competitiveness, Japan had less reason to oppose liberalization and correspondingly greater reason to support a liberal international order. Komiya and Itoh succinctly sum up the reasons for Japan's growing confidence.

> Japan's comparative advantage today is based on such factors as organizational and managerial skills, intelligent and cooperative labor, an efficient use of information, and flexibility in shifting resources from one sector to another. Such technologies in a wider sense are of a versatile character and can be applied over a fairly wide range of manufacturing industries. It appears that Japan will lead other countries in this kind of technology and hence in a fairly wide range of sophisticated manufacturing industries for some time to come.
>
> Since such technologies can be applied to many new industries in which technological innovation is taking place or for which the world demand is increasing rapidly, and since Japan has a severe comparative disadvantage in industries dependent on natural resources and land, free multilateral world trade will be most advantageous for Japan.[28]

In sum, to perceptive leaders of the business community and to bureaucrats in some (but by no means all) of the ministries, Japan's stake in the continuation of the international order prescribed a fundamental change in its foreign policy.

Ōhira's advisers were among the first groups to give coherent expression to this belief. The first of the nine groups reporting, the Research Group on Foreign Economic Policy, asserted, for example:

> Now a major economic power in its own right, Japan cannot be allowed to accept the existing international environment and concentrate solely upon how best to exploit such environment. . . . Japan should take the lead in observing the GATT agreements and other rules of the international economic community. . . . The 1980s will require increasingly that Japan act on its own initiative.

The report, issued April 21, 1980, called for Japan on its own initiative to liberalize and to deregulate the economy, to restructure domestic industry to avoid beggar-thy-neighbor policies, and to stimulate domestic demand to avoid flooding foreign markets with exports. Subsequent research reports reiterated these themes. They were advocated not as altruistic policies but as policies that would serve Japan's own interests.[29]

Following on the heels of the Ōhira groups, other prominent economic advisory groups expressed similar views. One such influential group reporting in 1982 was the Long-Term Outlook Committee of the Economic Planning Agency. The committee was composed of 128 prominent economists, bureaucrats, and businessmen, with its chairman Ōkita Saburō, former foreign minister. Its report entitled "Japan in the Year 2000" had a declared purpose to contribute to the formation of a national consensus (*kokumin no gōi*) on internationalist themes: the end of catch-up, the consequent need for self-generated plans for the future, and Japan's own self-interest in maintaining an open international economic order.[30] During the early 1980s, such views gained ground in MITI, excluding some sections of the ministry with jurisdiction over industries still being protected.

In addition to the evolution of comparative advantage, another change in the structure of the Japanese economy that favored the new internationalism was the rapid rise in foreign direct investment (FDI) after 1985, when Japan became the world's leading net creditor. The benefits of FDI for Japan included new markets, lowered production costs, easing of protectionist pressures, and acquisition of benefits from the preferential policies of host governments. FDI required a greatly enhanced sensitivity, tact, and knowledge of foreign conditions and sensibilities. As a MITI advisory report put it:

> For direct investment to remain fruitful over the long run, close relations must be maintained with local [that is, foreign] employees, firms, and local society, and the investing firm must strive to contribute to the development of the host country. Care should be taken lest the locals feel that foreign ways are being imposed on them. If Japanese enterprises can blend into the local socioeconomic system and become an indispensable part of local society, then the host government will be much less likely to take measures prejudicial to the Japanese firms, because such measures would hurt the local economy as well. Negligence in such efforts will not only increase the risk of jeopardizing the investment but will draw a dark cloud over all of the firm's activities, including exports from Japan.[31]

In short, if the vastly expanding FDI were not implemented with the utmost care and finesse, it could jeopardize not only FDI but Japan's domestic economy itself. Therefore the MITI advisory report prescribed a list of internationalist precautions that firms engaged in FDI must follow so as not to provoke anti-Japanese sentiment:

1. Economic benefits of FDI must be appropriately distributed between the firm and the host country through joint ventures, stock offerings that incorporate local capital into the firm, and local reinvestment of profits.
2. Transfer of production skills and technologies congruent with the level of development of the host country should be promoted. This entails the training of core technicians from the host country in Japan and inculcating not only skills but also a deeper understanding of Japan.
3. A unified structure of the labor force must be established in the parent company and its local subsidiaries to provide incentives for local employees with superior management skills to advance and to remain with the firm, and to prevent local resentment of Japanese domination of all the key positions.
4. Care should be taken to avoid disruption of the social organization and values of the host country through aggressive and insensitive policies. The parent company must send abroad Japanese who are familar with local society in the host country.
5. The Japanese firm and its managers should participate in local social events and assist in charitable activities to smooth relations with the indigenous population.
6. To demonstrate reciprocity, direct investment in Japan must also be facilitated and encouraged. Although the Japanese are confident that most FDI will be from Japan to other countries because of the high level of Japanese technology, in some areas such as service industries, investment in Japan will be expanding and significant. Accordingly, Japanese markets will need to become more open to FDI.[32]

The new internationalism gained impetus not only from the growing strength of the economy as manifested in dramatic improvements of its comparative advantage and in overseas investment, but also from a new conception of Japan's future. Japan's new internationalism was based on a confident belief that the nation was destined by its unique economic, scientific, and cultural skills to be the pioneer of a new stage of technology and that this would project Japan into the role of global leadership. A tone of national pride clearly suffused the new internationalism as did an air of inevitability and technological determination. The 1986

MITI advisory report stated the premise: history teaches that leadership in a technological revolution also entails leadership of the international system. In the nineteenth century, England's pioneering role in the creation of steam and iron technology and its application to rail transport and ocean-going vessels laid the basis for the Pax Britannica; in the twentieth century, U.S. leadership in electric and chemical technology and its application to the automobile, airplane, and consumer durables laid the basis for the Pax Americana. In sum:

> In the past, major changes in the technological structure invariably wrought changes in the international system as a whole: the country which held the overwhelming advantage in a specific industry or a specific technology that was the key in the technological paradigm for the world's economic development in a given era became the leader of international society and took the initiative in the formation of the international order of that era.[33]

For Japan, in short, its century-long pursuit of stature among nations required one final, revolutionary step. In its own interest, it must set aside the narrow conception of national interest that had motivated it and replace it with a global perspective that would see Japan as a leader of the international system. As the world's most efficient and competitive economy, Japan had a powerful incentive to encourage and maintain the rules of a liberal open world economy. True nationalism for Japan was now the new internationalism. As MITI's report stated succinctly, "Japan cannot expect to grow or prosper unless the rest of the world grows and prospers."[34]

Tenets of the New Internationalism

Accordingly, the first principle of the new internationalism was that Japan must give support and leadership to the institutions of a liberal international system. This was urgent because Japanese perceived the U.S. leadership declining. Throughout the 1970s, the decline of the United States had been a common theme of public discourse. A major thesis of the Ōhira Research Group of Comprehensive National Security, which issued its report on July 2, 1980, was that

> the days are gone when Japan could count on [an international] system maintained single-handedly by the United States, be it in terms of military security, politics

and diplomacy, or the economy. Japan must now contribute to the maintenance and management of the system as an influential member of the free world. There has been a shift from a world of "Pax Americana" to the world of "peace maintained by shared responsibilities."[35]

The new internationalism believed, in light of the Reagan military buildup, that the United States would continue in the near term to provide military-security leadership but that the international economy would be supervised by a "collective management system." Japan must join other nations in providing the "public goods" required by the international system such as an open trading system, development assistance, expenditures on research and development, and lending agencies of last resort for nations facing massive debts. Although some internationalists, like Nakasone, believed that economics and politics could no longer be separated, the mainstream concluded that "Japan must not aim to be a hegemonic power preponderant in all fields—economic, military, and international political—but should define its role in the world primarily in terms of economic strength," following the examples of Venice, Holland, and other leading trading states in history. This role would entail active Japanese leadership to expand free trade and to promote coordination of international fiscal and monetary policy.[36]

A second fundamental tenet of the new internationalism was much more controversial because of the immediate threat it represented to institutions and social practices as well as to a vast array of private interests in Japan. This tenet was what the internationalists call

the commitment to harmonize national actions with global interests. This will necessitate reform and/or reorganization of political, economic, social, and educational and other domestic institutions. . . . These efforts . . . will no doubt be accompanied by considerable friction and turmoil, imposing severe strains on the nation. The responsibility of Japanese, in view of their country's position in the world, is to surmount these difficulties . . . and to cultivate a global perspective. . . . Needless to say, strong political leadership and popular support will be needed if Japan is to successfully shoulder these responsibilities.[37]

Harmonizing Japanese institutions with international practice recalled U.S. Commerce Secretary Baldrige's assertion to the Japanese: "You will have to change your culture." The century-long pursuit of equality with the West had left its mark on all of Japan's institutions. They were designed to promote a uniform and disciplined national effort to achieve this goal. They were also designed to insulate Japan from direct influence by foreign companies and individuals. To play the new role of international leader, Japan's economic, social, and educational institutions had to be made more open, flexible, tolerant of diversity, and responsible to the expectations of Japan's new status.

The new internationalism was thus addressing the difficult and controversial issue of international norms versus domestic autonomy. Formerly, adherence to the norms of a liberal open economic system meant maintaining nondiscriminatory tariffs and refraining from overt quotas on imports. The growth of interdependence of national economies, however, had increased the relevance of domestic social structures and economic policies to the smooth operation of a liberal international economy. As Gary R. Saxonhouse writes,

> The thrust of international economic diplomacy has moved from tariff to quotas and from quotas to standards, subsidies, and government procurement. The agenda for international economic harmony seems now to include the demand that much of the domestic affairs of participants in the international economic system should be governed by fully competitive, open, and contractual relationships.[38]

Probably more than any other single factor, the Japanese system had created this clash between domestic autonomy and international norms in international economic negotiations. "Western liberal societies," Robert Gilpin observes,

> find Japanese economic success particularly threatening because it is the first non-Western and nonliberal society to outcompete them. Whereas Western economies are based on belief in the superior efficiency of the free market and individualism, the market and the individual in Japan are not relatively autonomous but are deeply embedded in a powerful nonliberal culture and social system.[39]

Saxonhouse compiled a formidable list of distinctive Japanese economic institutions and policies that from an American if not from a West European perspective constituted an "illiberal" way of conducting economic affairs.[40]

To reform these institutions and practices would constitute a challenge to central features of Japanese culture, social relations, and political structure. The new internationalism sought a liberalization of institutions partly because they were remnants of the catch-up process, partly because they might inflame protectionist sentiment in other countries, and partly because liberalization would better qualify Japan for leadership.

The third fundamental tenet of the new internationalism was, as the MITI advisory report stressed, cultivation of "consciousness of the global community" or "internal internationalism." True internationalism meant not only institutional change; it required "a transformation of the national consciousness" to leave behind the old catch-up mentality and to prepare the Japanese for international leadership. The indispensable innovation that would transform Japan was a new liberal nationalism, which would have more open and universal characteristics than the traditional nationalism. Professor Ōtake has termed it an "internationalist nationalism" (*kokusaiteki nashonarisumu*).[41]

The internationalists believed that the global strategy of Japan to become a leader of the international system in the next century depended on the success of their agenda. As the 1986 MITI advisory report stressed, "Future Japanese affluence can only be achieved by participation in the international community. It is for its own benefit that Japan must make efforts at international exchange and to develop a global perspective."[42] In short, Japan's new internationalism was not to be an empty idealism; it was instead based on a new vision of Japan's future self-interest.

To accomplish the kind of shift of national purpose envisioned by the Ōhira commissions and by the other internationalists would be truly revolutionary, entailing a kind of Japanese perestroika, for such a shift would go contrary to the policies of the past century and the historical disposition of the Japanese people. It is by no means clear that a people can readily make such changes in their institutions, values, and patterns of behavior. Japan's unique cultural identity is not the only obstacle. The burden of Japan's own historical struggles to catch up with Western nations also constrained it from readily accomplishing this shift of national purpose and fulfilling the role of an international leader. For purposes of stark comparison, U.S. history gave the United States certain natural advantages that paved the way for it to be an international leader: the universal values that came out of the American Revolution, the continental abundance of resources, the geographical position that gave it free security in which to develop, and the historical struggles to assimilate different races and creeds. Ernest May wrote in the conclusion to his book on America's unplanned rise to world power at the beginning of this century, "Some nations achieve greatness; the United States had greatness thrust upon it."[43]

Japan's national experience had been quite the contrary. Stature among nations was a goal to be achieved; it was not bestowed. From the beginning of its modern century in 1868, Japan struggled for national power. Unlike other modern revolutions, Japan's did not give rise to universal values or an ideology of universal appeal. Instead it generated a nationalist struggle to gain equality with the West. National power was to be achieved by unremitting hard work, unity, and sacrifice. Self-reliance was essential, for Japan was surrounded by predatory imperial powers. "All countries beyond the seas are our enemies," Iwakura Tomomi wrote in 1869, describing the world Japan had entered to his fellow oligarchs.[44]

Japan's emergence in the 1980s as a world economic power was the outcome of this century-long, all-consuming struggle. Ōhira and the internationalists questioned whether the policies and practices of the nationalist struggle that were responsible for the successes of the past were ones to bring success to Japan in its new circumstances. The issue for them was not whether Japan would still be nationalist, still pursue its own national interests. That, after all, was the purpose of the nation-state. The issue, rather, was what form nationalism should take in the new circumstances of the late-twentieth century.

6

The Struggle to Reorient
Japanese Purpose

The task of reorienting Japanese purpose in accord with a broader conception of national interest was undertaken by Nakasone Yasuhiro during his five-year term (1982–1987) as prime minister. His term represented a marriage of the political nationalism that had opposed the Yoshida strategy since 1950 and the new internationalism that was a product of the neoconservative ideas articulated in the Ōhira commissions. Long known as a proponent of constitutional revision and Japanese rearmament, Nakasone came to office declaring that it was time to address hitherto taboo topics and "settle all accounts on postwar political issues" (*sengo seiji no sōkessan*). At the same time, as he raised the issues of political nationalism that had been largely suppressed since 1960, he surrounded himself with many of Ōhira's former advisers from business and academia. He was attracted by the broader conception of Japanese national interest advocated by the new internationalism and included it in his agenda.

Nakasone's adoption of the internationalist definition of Japanese purpose was attacked by the political opposition as a revival of nationalism in a new guise. The progressives called it "a new form of Japanese nationalism in the larger world environment" and a revival of prewar ideology "coming into existence through a dynamic integration of the recently emergent forms of industrial or enterprise nationalism and the more traditional or established forms of State-centered nationalism." While clothing their policies in the rhetoric of internationalism, the real goal of government and industrial leaders was "reaching an even higher and more

85

dominant position in the world marketplace." Progressive critics further castigated the reforms of the internationalists as constituting a plan for Japan to consolidate "the economic gains it has won over recent years and increase its already powerful advantages in the global economy." In short, it all added up to "Japan's ambition to rise to a position of singular importance and power in the twenty-first century."[1]

Nakasone had long been an outspoken nationalist. At the time of the Dulles-Yoshida negotiations, as a brash young Diet member less than half Yoshida's age, he made a bold protest against the prime minister's policy. The thirty-two-year-old Nakasone addressed a 7,000-word petition to General MacArthur asking for constitutional revision and an independent defense establishment. The supreme commander was said to have angrily brushed aside the petition; Nakasone, for his part, absented himself from the Diet's adoption proceedings for the Japan-U.S. security treaty.

Throughout the postwar decades, Nakasone held to a position of political nationalism. From the early days of his political career he advocated overturning the educational reforms imposed by the occupation and increasing the nationalist content of the curriculum. Nakasone advocated "a constitution drawn up independently by the Japanese people," termination of the security treaty, and conclusion of a genuine alliance with the United States on an equal footing. He served during 1970–1971 as director-general of the Japan Defense Agency (JDA) and used this position to draw attention to his views by having the JDA issue Japan's first defense white paper, which advocated his concept of a more "autonomous defense" (jishu bōei). Nakasone held this post only eighteen months, and little came of his hopes for establishing a more activist role in security affairs.[2]

Decades after the signing of the San Francisco Peace Treaty, Nakasone was still unhappy with the Yoshida Doctrine. He wrote in 1982:

> In hindsight one could argue that Prime Minister Yoshida's strategy represented, in its own way, a rational decision. By leaving Japan's defense to another country, he was able to reduce the defense burden, allowing the country to concentrate on rebuilding its devastated economy and reconstructing a stable democratic nation.
>
> Yet I cannot help but wonder, even now, about what might have happened had Japan made a different choice at that critical juncture. Ever since . . . I have made it one

of my political goals to transcend the so-called San Francisco system.[3]

As a measure of the confusion and disarray within the LDP, the party turned to this maverick for new leadership in 1982. Nakasone was an accidental prime minister—chosen, despite his opposition to the conservative mainstream policies, only after the factions were deadlocked over a successor to Suzuki, who had abruptly resigned.

The palpable nationalist mood of Japan at the beginning of the 1980s and the utter ineptness of Prime Minister Suzuki in handling the nation's foreign policy set the stage for Nakasone's emergence as the most imposing leader in foreign affairs that Japanese politics had produced since Yoshida more than thirty years earlier. A series of incidents of almost Gilbert-and-Sullivan character in the spring and summer of 1981 illustrated the strange, even arcane, aspects of the defense debate on the eve of Nakasone's ascent to the prime ministership. A joint communique issued by Prime Minister Suzuki and President Reagan, after their meeting in Washington, was widely criticized by the Japanese media for its use of the word "alliance" to describe the relationship between the two countries. Surprisingly, the prime minister himself joined in the criticism of the communique after his return to Tokyo. Next, Itō Masayoshi, the foreign minister, resigned, taking responsibility for the drafting of the communique.

Hard on the heels of this event, former ambassador Edwin Reischauer gave an interview to the *Mainichi* newspaper in which he casually remarked that U.S. nuclear-armed warships had been calling at Japanese ports for twenty years. Opposition parties and the media charged that this practice contravened the government's three nonnuclear principles of not manufacturing, possessing, or permitting the entry of nuclear weapons. The government, however, maintained that the security treaty provided for prior consultation before introduction of nuclear weapons was permitted and since there had been no consultation, introduction had not occurred. Clearly the Japanese government did not want to face or to resolve the issue and preferred to leave it wrapped in ambiguities. One prominent strategic thinker, Sase Masamori, observed that if Japan continued to rely on the U.S.-Japan security treaty while denying its military implications, and to rely on the U.S. nuclear umbrella while not allowing passage of nuclear weapons through its waters, then it must be reckoned an "international eccentric" (*kokusai-teki henjin*) whose behavior defied common sense, a country that "makes its way through international society peddling its special national characteristics."[4]

Nakasone's Grand Design

Shortly after Nakasone became prime minister, a member of the brain trust he had inherited from the Ōhira commissions, Kōyama Ken'ichi, wrote that Japan needed a "grand design" for its future—a vision to take the place of the progrowth consensus that heretofore inspired the people. Kōyama was one of the advisers who helped push Nakasone beyond his old political nationalism to a more forward-looking view and a broader conception of Japanese national interest. Kōyama argued that the conditions that had made for the success of the Yoshida strategy had changed. Japan had caught up with the West economically and technologically; the Pax Americana was in decline; and Japanese policy was the object of foreign criticism on all sides. It was no longer appropriate to adhere to the pragmatic, opportunistic, and reactive policies of the past. Japan must increasingly play the role of leader in the international system and set forth its own objectives and principles and policies.[5]

Nakasone was determined to create a new national consensus, a grand design for an activist foreign policy to supplant the Yoshida Doctrine, which he always regarded as passive and demeaning. To do so meant confronting the mainstream of the party and the bureaucracy. As prime minister, therefore, he set out to expand the usual limits of his office, to do an end around against the party and the bureaucracy, to defeat the Yoshida Doctrine, and to achieve a thorough transformation of Japan's international role. He would not wait for the bottom-up approach, whereby consensus wells up from below, which he said frustrates the kind of bold, institutional reform and policy changes needed to achieve fundamental reorientation of national opinion.

Three characteristics distinguished Nakasone's style of leadership in contrast to his predecessors:

1. He adopted a high-profile, top-down, some would say presidential-style, leadership. Nakasone projected a strong personal element. As he said, "In the age of mass democracy, the leader bears all the responsibilities. The leader must write the script himself, be the lead actor, do the choreography, and plan the PR."[6]

2. He used the foreign policy responsibilities of his office to maximum advantage, engaging in a steady succession of diplo-

matic forays. Though often more rhetoric than reality, more show than substance, more promise than performance, these diplomatic activities gave Japanese foreign policy a more activist cast.

3. Nakasone appointed an unusual number of government commissions, semiprivate study councils, and private advisory boards to highlight his pet proposals and to bring forth largely predetermined policy recommendations. The Diet has no say in the appointment of members to these private groups. But even when official ad hoc councils were set up, Nakasone found ways to influence their composition. He chose prominent academics, opinion leaders, and businessmen whose views were sympathetic to his own for advisory panels to deal with such controversial issues as defense, education, the Yasukuni Shrine, and the structure of the economy. In this way, he tried to shape the policy agenda and to invest his ideas with the legitimacy that came from the support of distinguished panels. After his party's landslide victory in July 1986, the prime minister effused to an admirer, "For the first time in Japanese political history, I was able to bypass the Government and party bureaucrats and take my case directly to the Japanese people. They responded as people responded to President Kennedy in 1960. The political scene will not be the same again."[7]

We can discern four major tenets of Nakasone's grand design to reorient Japan's national purpose and to establish a new national consensus in place of the Yoshida Doctrine:

1. Japan would no longer be a follower nation.
2. Japan would be prepared for global leadership by being remade into an international state.
3. A new liberal nationalism would be based on the concept of the country's national interests beyond traditional nationalism.
4. Japan would assume an active role in global strategic affairs.

A New Vision

The first dimension offered a new vision of Japan's future: the conviction that Japan should no longer play the part of a follower nation. As Nakasone wrote on the eve of assuming the prime ministership, "The first necessity is a change in our thinking. Having 'caught up,' we must now expect others to try to catch up with us. We must seek out a new path for ourselves and open it up ourselves."[8] The Japanese should recognize that they were destined to become the world's economic, scientific, and technological leaders in the next century. The belief that Japan would lead a new wave of revolutionary technological innovation in the world in the twenty-first century was widely held, but Nakasone's circle argued that this scientific leadership would require political leadership as well.

This conviction of a rendezvous with destiny for Japan in the twenty-first century was a recurrent theme in the Ōhira commissions. Nakasone gave strong expression to this belief and drew distinctive conclusions from it. In particular, he seized on the vision of a new stage of human and technological development called *jōhō shakai*, the information society, that was a favorite concept of the commissions. Addressing the Diet on February 6, 1984, shortly after his reelection, he spoke of "the unknown challenges of the twenty-first century." What was striking about his vision was his stress on "the achievement of a sophisticated information society [as] an important strategic element in medium and long-term economic development for the twenty-first century." He promised to promote policies and to "establish a national consensus on what we want of the information society and to respond appropriately on a broad range of fields including frontier technology research and development." This optimistic image of the Japanese future and of its revolutionary implications captivated the prime minister and his advisers. In a little-noticed address to the Japan Society in New York, following the Williamsburg summit, Nakasone envisioned Japan's future development in

> the electronics and communication technology necessary to sustain an information society. . . . The achievement of the information society seems primary, since it goes beyond changes in the production structure and . . . will mean the unfolding of a new and unprecedented stage of development. This may take twenty or even thirty years to realize, yet we should not let the long time span deter us.

Several ambitious and high-visibility projects receiving official encouragement and sponsorship became symbols of the drive toward an information society. These included a variety of new media such as the Information Network System (INS), a new telecommunication network pushed by Nippon Telegraph and

Telephone; Community Antenna Television (CATV); and the Character and Telephone Access Information Network (CAPTAIN), providing vast amounts of home information. The fifth-generation computer received international attention, but a far more ambitious project was MITI's plan to develop "technopolises" to diffuse the most advanced technologies into regional centers as the backbone of the Japanese economy in the twenty-fist century.

To extend the work of the Ōhira commissions, the Ministry of Finance in 1984 organized a project of impressive proportions to study the "next stage of civilization," which Japan was thought to be leading. The MOF established thirty-nine teams of experts, some 470 experts in all, from various academic disciplines, industry, and government to undertake research on various aspects of the new civilization. Many of the team leaders were among the prime minister's circle of advisers. One of the key thinkers, economist Murakami Yasusuke, in a series of essays described the emergence of a new phase of industrial civilization following the oil crisis of 1973. This "twenty-first-century system, the system of so-called high technology" would bring with it an entirely new paradigm: novel behavior patterns and modes in using the new technology, new groups of specialists in producing and operating the new technology, as well as a hitherto unfamiliar set of varied infrastructures, including large and multipurpose cables, huge data bases, a new educational system, and a transformed social system. Murakami observed in January 1984 that "there are more than a few people who consider the call for an 'information society' a simple dream, but broadly speaking history is moving in that direction. If the Japanese people are hesitant, it is inevitable that someone else will provide the move toward an information society." The question for the coming decades, he mused, seemed to be, "Will Japan be able to mature as a completely new leading nation, originating not from Europe or America?"[9]

This image of Japan's future as a leader of a new phase of human progress was in marked contrast to the premise of the Yoshida Doctrine, which had fashioned a progrowth consensus to concentrate Japan's energy and resources so that it might catch up to the West. Assessing Japan's progress three decades later, Nakasone believed that it was time to replace Western industrial society as the image of Japan's future with new goals of Japan's own making.

Japan as an International State

The second dimension of Nakasone's grand design was to prepare for global leadership by remaking Japan into an international state (*kokusai kokka*). This entailed reform of Japan's institutions to harmonize them with international expectations. The century-long pursuit of equality with the West influenced the shape of all Japan's important institutions. They were designed to promote a uniform and disciplined national effort to achieve rapid growth. The economy included many institutions that from a Western perspective constituted an illiberal way of conducting economic affairs: government industrial policy, cartels and other forms of collusion, a closed distribution system, enterprise groups (*keiretsu*), forced placement of government debt, noncompetitive public sector procurement, tax preferences, and encouragement of savings to promote exports. These and other distinctive institutional arrangements that were defended by an array of powerful domestic interests had become the subject of intense foreign criticism because of Japan's rising trade surpluses.

Nakasone sought a liberalization of institutions partly because he was convinced that they were often inefficient remnants of the catch-up process, partly because they were inflaming protectionist sentiment in other countries, and partly because, by opening up the nation's institutions and practices, liberalization would better qualify Japan for international respect and leadership. Nakasone's experience as head of the Administrative Reform Commission (*Rinchō*) had clearly influenced him. In a speech at the outset of *Rinchō*, he said his goal was to bring about the third major social reform in the history of modern Japan, comparable to the Meiji Restoration and the postwar reforms. The achievements of *Rinchō* fell far short of this goal, although over the next several years its recommendations did succeed in creating a blueprint for a leaner, more streamlined, better rationalized administration. Progress was made in the privatization of public corporations, inducing greater competition and generally loosening some aspects of bureaucratic control of the economy, which had been a significant part of the catch-up effort.

By 1985, however, Nakasone faced a mounting crisis with Japan's trading partners. The trade surplus with the United States was approaching $50 billion; an economic summit was scheduled in Tokyo in the spring of 1986, preceded by a meeting in Washington with President Reagan. The outcome of these events would influence the forthcoming popular elections and the party decision about the extension of his term.

In response to this crisis, he resorted to a private advisory council—in many ways, the most bold of his familiar methods of dealing with a national issue. In the autumn of 1985, Nakasone handpicked a seventeen-member private council, known as the Advisory Group on Economic Structural Adjustment for International Harmony, chaired by the former governor of the Bank of Japan, Maekawa Haruo, to recommend measures to deal with the trade imbalances. To ensure the appropriate conclusions, he attended all but one of the group's meetings. Much of the party and the bureaucracy were left in the dark. In April 1986, on the eve of his trip to Washington and the Tokyo Summit, the group unveiled its so-called Maekawa Report.[10] "The time has come," it said, "for Japan to make a historic transformation in its traditional lifestyle." It acknowledged that trade surpluses had to change "for Japan to become a truly international state," and it promised expansion of domestic demand through promotion of housing construction and urban redevelopment, change in preferential tax treatment for savings, increased imports, and a five-day workweek. Nakasone was subject to a barrage of criticism for this end run and for the self-contradictions and lack of specific proposals in the report.

In Washington Nakasone presented the Maekawa Report as a Japanese commitment to restructure the economy, but back in Tokyo he retreated and referred to it simply as a "target Japan will do its best to meet in the medium to long term."[11] A second Maekawa Report issued a year later, in April 1987, extended the commitment to restructure the economy, to lessen economic friction with other countries, and to play a leadership role in the world economy. It recommended further changes to shift to domestic-led growth: reform of the distribution system, removal of barriers to trade in a number of industries, measures to relieve third world debt, and a greater role in providing development assistance. Nakasone had set a monumental, even revolutionary, task for the nation. As a report of a MITI advisory group that included Nakasone partisans observed in 1986,

> These efforts . . . will no doubt be accompanied by considerable friction and turmoil, imposing severe internal strains on the nation. The responsibility of Japanese, in view of their country's position in the world, is to surmount these difficulties . . . and to cultivate a global perspective. . . . Needless to say, strong political leadership and popular support will be needed if Japan is to successfully shoulder these responsibilities.

The report stressed that a restructuring of the Japanese economy so as to harmonize its institutions with international expectations "entails a shift in emphasis away from short-term national interests and toward long-term global interests" of Japan.[12]

A New Liberal Nationalism

The third dimension of Nakasone's grand design was his advocacy of a new liberal nationalism based on a conception of Japan's national interests that transcended that of traditional Japanese nationalism. If Japan was to assume the role of global leader, it was no longer appropriate to suppress political nationalism, as the Yoshida strategy did. Though subject to continuing criticism by his political opposition as a proponent of militarism and pre-war-style nationalism, Nakasone professed a more cosmopolitan ideal. He argued for an appreciation of Japan's special strengths and abilities within an international framework that combined national pride with appreciation for the cultures and traditions of other nations.

At an LDP seminar in Shizuoka, September 22, 1986, he told party members:

> In order to advance along the course of an international state, what is more important as one aspect of this transformation is that we Japanese must know Japan itself. In other words, this is often called identity, and this is the identity argument. Know not thyselves, and comparison and contrast with other countries cannot be made. Accordingly as one aspect of this concept of pro-gressing toward an international state, to know ourselves means that Japan must be studied with the same energy that we expend on becoming an international state in the sense of contributing to world peace and prosperity.[13]

Nakasone envisioned the emergence of a new Japanese na-tional character, that is, a new Japanese personality bespeaking the role of international leader. The Japanese people must acquire appropriate new qualities that would command the respect of other peoples. Charles de Gaulle dismissed Prime Minister Ikeda as a "mere transistor salesman"; Henry Kissinger privately de-rided the Japanese as "little Sony salesmen," or "small and petty bookkeepers," whose diplomatic documents were nothing more than trading ledgers. Because they were not part of the interna-tional power equation, Kissinger was said to have disdained them as "prosaic, obtuse, unworthy of his sustained attention." Japa-nese were highly sensitive to being labeled "economic animals" and hence were stung by a 1979 European Commission report that said:

> [Japan's trade expansion was due to the] hard work, discipline, corporate loyalties, and management skills of

a crowded, highly competitive island people only recently emerged from a feudal past, a country of worka-
holics who live in what Westerners would regard as little
more than rabbit hutches. . . . [There is] as much propensity to import as there would be carnival spirit on a rainy
Sunday morning in Glasgow.[14]

Nakasone believed that the Japanese must attain a sense of self-
confidence and national pride. Modern history left the Japanese
as a people with a legacy of personality traits that must be
overcome. The catch-up effort compelled the Japanese to borrow
large quantities of knowledge and institutions from Western countries to replace the inherited wisdom and values of their own
culture. To the Japanese with their culturally ingrained sense of
hierarchy and status, this demeaning condition created a peculiar
sense of inferiority and loss of pride.

Defeat and occupation by a foreign country further undermined pride in the national heritage. The postwar generation was
left with an uncertain view of the nation. The writer Hasegawa
Michiko (b. 1945), for example, described her generation as struggling to find a Japanese identity through reexamination of the
meaning of the Pacific war: "Those of us born in the immediate
postwar years see ourselves as children born of darkness." They
were taught that Japanese history culminating in the Pacific war
had led to disaster. Cut off from their past, they lacked a sense of
pride as Japanese: "Who are we? How can we be ourselves? In
order to make these simple questions meaningful, we must once
more review the significance of the war."[15] Nakasone was representative of the view of the wartime generation (senchū ha), which
was critical of the postwar materialism and the failure to formulate
any sense of national purpose in the pursuit of economic ends.
The late Yoshida Mitsuru, whose writings often expressed the
wartime generation's view, put it this way: "High economic
growth is not bad in itself; what is bad is that the Japanese have
no sense of the ends to which they wish to apply the power
brought about by high economic growth."[16]

Nakasone sought "a transformation of the national consciousness" so as to leave behind the old mentality and to prepare
young Japanese for international leadership. Reform of the educational system was urgent because the children starting school in
the 1980s would begin their careers in the twenty-first century.
Such reform was a key part of Nakasone's desire to overhaul
institutions and to make Japan an international state. He attempted to bypass the Ministry of Education, which he decided

was too tradition-minded to share his vision. Capitalizing on a widespread sense of malaise in the education system, Nakasone persuaded the Diet to establish the Ad Hoc Council on Education as a supracabinet advisory body to the prime minister on August 21, 1984—another example of his use of commissions to get across his ideas. He filled a substantial number of positions in the twenty-five-person panel with those whose views coincided with his own, including many of his own brain trust; Nakasone passed over representatives of the Japan Teachers' Union, whose views epitomized the postwar attitudes toward education. Nonetheless, he had to compromise with the Ministry of Education and its allies in the LDP to get the Diet to pass the enabling legislation for the council. This compromise subsequently made it all but impossible for Nakasone to achieve much of his education reform agenda.[17]

The Council on Education Reform undertook a three-year program of deliberations that led to a final set of conclusions by the summer of 1987. Nakasone's ideas of education reform were influenced by leaders of international business in Japan. A study group, the Kyoto Group for the Study of Global Issues, established by Matsushita Kōnosuke, one of the nation's most prominent business leaders, argued boldly for steps to loosen bureaucratic controls over education; its standardization had become a dead weight inhibiting the production of the more diverse and creative work force that the economy would need in the twenty-first century. Nakasone's partisans on the council took aim at a school structure characterized by standardization, centralization, and insulation from international influences. The purpose was to liberalize and to deregulate the educational system so as to permit greater diversity, flexibility, and even competition among schools. The prime minister therefore appointed proponents of liberalization, such as Kōyama Ken'ichi and former MITI vice minister Amaya Naohiro, a leader of the Kyoto Group, to key positions in the education council.

Nakasone's partisans said that the catch-up effort had required intense work, uniformity, unquestioning adherence to a set curriculum, and a stress on rote memory work. As a result, "respect for individuality, freedom, autonomy, self-responsibility, and humane values . . . tended to be ignored." The second report of the council said that "instead of mental and cultural values, the Japanese people have been mainly seeking such tangible values as profits, salaries, enrollment at colleges, gross national product, and market shares." What was required of the Japanese character in the twenty-first century was, first, a "broad mind, sound body, and rich creativity" and, second, "the spirit of freedom, autonomy, and civicmindedness."[18] These qualities were intended to contribute to creativity and greater diversity of individual talent so that Japan could produce the new ideas and genius required of world leadership.

Nakasone's advisers argued that the existing educational system was structured to promote the progrowth consensus. "During the stage when Japan was still catching up," observed Amaya,

> companies welcomed a mass produced supply of workers equipped with a uniform, homogeneous education. The resounding success of total quality control is closely tied to the uniform educational background and ability of Japanese workers. The big question now is whether what has succeeded in the twentieth century will also lead to success in the twenty-first century.[19]

Nakasone's circle wanted a shift from a single-track system to a diversity of schools; a loosening of the requirements for licensing and accreditation of schools in both secondary and higher education; greater latitude for competing teaching methods, curriculum, and teacher qualifications; and consideration of a wider range of achievement than simple test scores in school admissions and company hiring policies. Kōyama went further and suggested a radical reorganization of the Ministry of Education. The desired result of such institutional change was greater individuality and creativity among the graduates of the system.

Still more important in preparing Japan for leadership in the new century was the opening up of schools to international influences. Nakasone and his advisers wanted to remove obstacles to the hiring of foreign teachers and acceptance of foreign students so as to improve foreign language instruction and to enhance Japanese understanding of other cultures. "Our schools," Kōyama wrote, "do not train people for international communication by nurturing their ability to express themselves, to debate, and to interact with people of other countries."[20] By the same measure, Nakasone enthusiastically promoted ideas to facilitate understanding by foreigners of the Japanese people and their culture. He suggested a center for Japanology and programs to bring vast numbers of foreign students to Japan.

The education report stressed formation of "Japanese identity in a global context." This meant a firm sense of Japanese traditions and strengths but not in the exclusive sense of prewar nationalism.

> It is essential for Japanese not only to be assertive about the distinctive character of Japanese society and culture

[but also to] deeply understand the excellence of other cultures in the world. Although one is expected to love Japan as a Japanese, he must avoid judging things on the basis of narrow nationalistic interests only, and try to build his character with a broad international and global perspective that covers all humanity.[21]

The desired product of a reformed education would be a new self-confident Japanese, at home in the world, not clinging to other Japanese when abroad, but rather communicating easily with foreigners and understanding their mores.

MITI's report on "Japan in the Global Community," the product of an advisory committee including several Nakasone partisans, was issued in April 1986. It held out hope for the early development of the desired personality traits, which it said were already evident in Japanese history but had simply been overshadowed by the characteristics required by rapid catch-up. Westerners and Japanese alike have stereotyped the Japanese as quintessential organization men. "Deeply loyal to their organizations and highly skilled in group management and human relations, organization men excel at steadfastly pursuing a given goal." Their "solidarity, efficiency and devotion to detail . . . helped propel Japan to its present prosperity." Such stereotypes however ignored an

utterly different aspect of the Japanese character, one of adventurousness and strong individualistic leadership. The founders of many corporations, who concern themselves more with new ideas and product innovation, belong to this group. They excel in individual creativity. . . . They are often curious about a wide variety of activities, and more internationalist than parochial in outlook.

Examples offered were Oda Nobunaga, whose genius was to create a new social order; the Meiji entrepreneurs; and maverick leaders of certain postwar businesses such as Sony and Honda. The report therefore concluded with optimism: "If present-day Japanese come to regard the adventurous personality type . . . as an appropriate model, perhaps internationalization can be achieved relatively painlessly by switching emphasis from one of the personality types within the traditional culture to another."[22]

Nakasone was convinced that self-confidence must begin with an appreciation of traditional institutions and history. He therefore attached importance to the issue of the Yasukuni Shrine. Many postwar prime ministers had visited Yasukuni, the Shinto shrine that honors the spirits of the war dead in the modern era. Going back to Yoshida, prime ministers had visited in an official capacity during the autumn festival, but none had made such a visit on the day commemorating the end of World War II. Nakasone's predecessors had visited as private persons on August 15. Families of the war dead, a powerful LDP constituency, had long lobbied for restoration of the shrine's prewar status. In 1984 an LDP committee declared that formal worship at the shrine by the prime minister and cabinet ministers was constitutional.

For Nakasone, the issue assumed great symbolic importance. It offered a symbolic way of putting the war aside as a source of national shame and embarrassment and returning to traditional reverence for the spirits of the war dead. At an LDP seminar at Karuizawa in the summer of 1985, he said the Yasukuni issue was important because it showed the gratitude of the people for the sacrifices made by their forebears. It was time to achieve a consensus on this issue so that "approaching the twenty-first century, the Japanese state and the Japanese people can walk proudly in the world" for "on the one hand Japan must become an international state but at the same time it is important to reestablish Japan's identity."[23]

To deal with this delicate subject, he again had recourse to a private advisory panel for a recommendation on the constitutional issue before the fortieth anniversary of the end of the war. But even members of his handpicked panel could not agree on the issue; he had to instruct them to paper over their internal differences. The final report was phrased so as to imply a consensus in favor of official worship. On August 15, 1985, Nakasone became the first prime minister to offer prayers in his official capacity on the day commemorating the end of the war. He also made a contribution from official funds. Fifteen cabinet ministers and 172 LDP Diet members joined Nakasone.

Remaking national character was not so easy a task as Nakasone and his partisans on the education council seemed to assume. In the first place, the effort was controversial. Both at home and abroad, there was a great deal of suspicion that he intended a revival of prewar nationalism. His worship at Yasukuni evoked official protests and student demonstrations in China and Korea. So serious was this reaction that he absented himself from the shrine a year later, in 1986. Despite the charges of his opposition, Nakasone's views were distinct from prewar nationalism. His views represented a more forward-looking nationalism: less narrow, xenophobic, and inward looking, less based on old values.

His nationalism was more urban, cosmopolitan, and middle class. It did not grow out of inferiority, as prewar nationalism did, or out of resentment at being behind the West in the production of modern science and technology, or out of resentment at being influenced by the values and institutions of another culture. It grew out of pride in Japanese achievements, the international acclaim they had brought, and self-confidence in the future. Above all, Nakasone's nationalism was based on the realization that it was now in Japan's national interest, as a new leading nation, to be more internationalist.

Remaking national character was also hard because old habits of thought and behavior die hard. To achieve the kind of open, balanced, liberal nationalism that Nakasone advocated entailed overcoming the old way of looking at the world in hierarchical terms and of exalting the Japanese race (*minzoku*) in the instinctive, provincial terms of the past. Nakasone himself sometimes slipped up in praising the homogeneity of the Japanese. In the autumn of 1986, he had to apologize formally to the American people for his slighting remarks about their minorities. These remarks were part of a talk to an LDP seminar in Shizuoka, September 22, 1986, in which he was boasting of the achievements of the Japanese as a "high-level information society":

> And there is no country which puts such diverse information so accurately into the ears of its people. It has become a very intelligent society. Against the likes of America it is by far so, when seen from averages.
>
> In America there are many blacks, Puerto Ricans, and Mexicans, and seen on an average, America's per capita level of intelligence, as gained through education and the mass media is still extremely low. Because Japan is such a dense, vibrant society, a high-level information society, a highly educated society, a society in which people are so vibrant, unless our party's politics continually progress to suit the people's appetite for knowledge/information/intelligence, our party will falter.[24]

That Nakasone himself revealed a lack of balance in his nationalism is a measure of how difficult the transformation of values will be for the nation. Commenting on his remarks, a leading Japanese editor wrote:

> Deep down, a majority of the Japanese people agreed with their prime minister's assessment that the Japanese society is at a "higher level" in certain aspects. The

Japanese belief in their own superiority seems to be more deeply ingrained than ever because of their ability to produce superb industrial products and high technology. . . . Japanese are a people of great contradiction. While the Japanese appear to have been prostrated before America, deep in their heart they have a certain enmity toward Americans. They look down on fellow Asians, but cannot abandon an obligatory feeling of affinity toward them. They are proud to be the world's leading economic power, but are not convinced if they are rich and strong.[25]

An Active Global Role

A fourth dimension of Nakasone's grand design, and the most controversial, was his determination to adopt an active role in strategic affairs. When he came to office in 1982, Japanese foreign policy was in disarray because of the weak and vacillating policies of his predecessor. From the moment he became prime minister, Nakasone used the diplomatic responsibilities of his office to try to undermine the Yoshida Doctrine and to undo the impression of a politically passive Japan. He made an unprecedented trip to Seoul and approved a long-term governmental loan that the Koreans explicitly linked to the strategic defense of Japan. Subsequently, in a series of bold public statements on strategic issues during his extraordinary visit to Washington in January 1983, Nakasone proclaimed a more activist Japanese role in the alliance. At the eleventh hour, before leaving for Washington, he elicited cabinet approval of the transfer of purely military technology to the United States in what symbolized a major modification of the three principles on arms exports.

In Washington he unleashed a series of rhetorical flourishes that implied strategic commitments that far exceeded Japan's capacity. Japan, he said, should aim for "complete and full control" of the strategic straits controlling the Sea of Japan "so that there should be no passage of Soviet submarines and other naval activities in time of emergency." Going still further, Nakasone said that Japan should be "a big aircraft carrier" (ōkina koku bokan)—his official translator interpolated this with the colorful phrase "an unsinkable aircraft carrier" (fuchin kubō)—to prevent penetration of the Soviet Backfire bombers into Japanese airspace. Fulfillment of this capability would require a large-scale military buildup that would far exceed the existing limitation of 1 percent of GNP on defense spending. Finally, he repeated statements he had made in Tokyo that there should be no taboos against discussion of constitutional revision; he added, "The Constitution is a very delicate issue and I have in mind a very long-range timetable, so to speak, but I would not dare mention it even in our Diet."[26] This bravado performance won the admiration of President Reagan and began a warm relationship that suited the needs of both leaders.

On a steady schedule of foreign visits, Nakasone made maximum use of these occasions in foreign capitals and at summits to convey a sense of dynamism that was unprecedented in the postwar era. As the 1986 election triumph indicated, his assertiveness had popular appeal. A *Mainichi* reporter observed after the election:

> A "strong Japan" was the leitmotif of Prime Minister Nakasone Yasuhiro's campaign. . . . Following the premier as he stumped the nation, I was struck by the enthusiastic response he aroused whenever he appealed to national pride. . . . His repeated references to "Nippon," a word with patriotic overtones, seemed to mesmerize the audience. "I am proud of the great nation Japan has become in the forty years since World War II," he continued. "As Japan's leader, I can talk with François Mitterrand or Ronald Reagan as an equal." . . . Judging from crowd reactions the secret of Nakasone's appeal lies in his ability to stir latent national pride and patriotism.[27]

Nakasone determined to break through the 1 percent barrier by appointing a private advisory panel on national security affairs to bring forth what he was confident would be a realist appraisal of Japan's defense needs. (This had been attempted once before when the Ōhira Commission on Comprehensive National Security Study Group proposed in 1980 a steady increase of defense expenditure, but the recommendation was soon forgotten in the Suzuki administration.) Nakasone's eleven-member Research Committee on Peace Problems (*Heiwa Mondai Kenkyūkai*) reported to the prime minister in December 1984 that the 1 percent ceiling on defense spending had outlived its validity and the 1976 defense buildup guidelines were inadequate; it urged an accelerated defense buildup. Privately it was known that even though the panel was personally chosen by the prime minister, its members were divided over the issue. Several were reluctant to take the strong stance of the majority and were reportedly prepared to offer a minority view, but Nakasone insisted on a unified conclusion.

In September 1985, armed with the committee's recommendations, the cabinet announced plans to abolish the 1 percent ceiling on the defense budget. But Nakasone had misjudged his ability to persuade the faction leaders in the LDP to support him. Opposition from former prime ministers Fukuda Takeo and Suzuki forced Nakasone to back down on this occasion. After further cajoling, Nakasone finally had his way—but only by a hair's breadth. In December 1986, the cabinet decided on a 1987 defense allocation that would exceed 1 percent of the projected GNP—by four one-thousandths of a percentage point.

While the tangible achievements of Nakasone in establishing a more activist foreign policy were limited and often symbolic, he did succeed in influencing the public debate and in creating greater receptivity to a more forthright alignment of Japan with the Western allies. He challenged the Yoshida strategy and justifications of Japan's withdrawn international behavior that rely on Article 9 (the nonbelligerency clause) of the constitution, the nuclear allergy, the three nonnuclear principles, the legacy of postwar pacifism, and other such explanations of Japan's exceptional status. Nakasone continued to state the importance of constitutional revision. During a Socialist interpellation in the Diet on October 16, 1985, for example, he maintained that reevaluation of the constitution was an essential priority for Japan as it approached the twenty-first century. As a matter of political strategy, he did not press the case during his tenure.

Nevertheless, the public's attitude toward the security treaty had by many measures become much more supportive since the late 1970s. One relatively little noticed result was a sharply increased level and sophistication of joint military training with forces from the United States and other Pacific nations. In 1986 Japan was the most active participant in the multilateral Rimpac exercises. Further reflection of this trend was the government's decision to participate in the strategic defense initiative, which, however, modest, would have been unthinkable in pre-Nakasone days.

Nakasone's Limited Success

Nakasone set a daunting task for himself. He challenged not only the mainstream views of his party but the underlying factors responsible for the reactive nature of the Japanese state as well. As an alternative to the Yoshida strategy, which consciously chose a dependency relationship with the United States, Nakasone formulated a vision of an activist Japan capable of world leadership, engaged in international political-strategic issues, participating in its own defense, possessing its own goals and values and objectives, and reshaping its institutions for the role of global leader. He addressed the psychological inhibitions that made the Yoshida strategy not only a shrewd but also a comfortable policy. To overcome the negative identity that the Japanese held of themselves in the aftermath of defeat, occupation, and international condemnation, Nakasone tried to transform the national consciousness by cultivating a balance between national pride and understanding of other traditions. To deal with cultural restraints such as the reliance on consensus building, he set forth his own agenda and pressed it with a forceful and direct personal style unusual in Japanese politics. Finally, to deal with systemic immobilism induced by an entrenched bureaucracy and factional competition, he resorted to advisory panels to go around the system and to highlight his program.

Nakasone's strategy met with limited successes. It modified the Yoshida Doctrine by making changes around the edges. His principal achievement was to articulate a new vision of Japan's role in the world. The actual accomplishments in changing the strategy were modest. He brought a new realism to the defense debate, and he committed Japan to greater cooperation with the Western allies. Nakasone modified, even if only in a limited way, such parts of the Yoshida strategy as the principles on arms exports and the 1 percent ceiling.

More than the words of this colorful prime minister was required to change a doctrine and a system that had been so successful in the recent past. The balance of power in Japanese politics was still with the adherents of the Yoshida strategy. Although Japan's international circumstances had been dramatically transformed since Yoshida's day, the strategy had proved its worth. Important elements of the political system continued to support it for their own reasons. They bought into part of Nakasone's grand design, for they also envisioned nothing less than Japanese global leadership in economic and technological development, the pioneering of a new technocratic society—in short, world leadership in the nonmilitary aspects of the international system. They believed that the importance of military power in international relations was declining because of the advent of nuclear weapons, increased economic interdependency, and a growing global consciousness.

Kōsaka Masataka, probably the most representative intellectual spokesman for the LDP mainstream, argued against any reorientation of Japanese foreign policy. In a 1985 essay he stressed the advantages of avoiding a national ideology and of maintaining a flexible pragmatism. Against those, like Nakasone, who held that Japan should bear a greater share of the military burden in support of the Western allies, Kōsaka offered the following arguments:

1. Because of the stalemate between the two nuclear superpowers, the positive uses of military power were few.

2. Since protecting Japan and maintaining peace in the Pacific were in America's own national interest, "it may not be necessary for us to pay a large share of the cost."

3. Since Japan was a source of essential credit and exports to the United States, the Japanese-American relationship could not easily be broken even if Japan contributed no more militarily.

Kōsaka implied that every effort must be made to maintain the Yoshida Doctrine. He recognized this created "a serious identity problem for the nation." But Japan, in its own best interests, must "preserve an indomitable spiritual strength without having any clear-cut and explicit principles." This argument was the antithesis of Nakasone's grand design.[28]

7

The Burdens of History

By the end of the 1980s, the new internationalism envisioned by the Ōhira Research Groups at the beginning of the decade had met with only limited successes. Nakasone left office in 1987 with a wry remark that the outcome of his grand design to transform Japan's international role was "yet to be seen."[1] The most egregious features of a closed economy, the formal barriers, had been largely laid aside. Whether because of foreign pressure or self-interest or the demonstrable strength of its economy, Japan dismantled some mercantilist policies. "By the mid-1980s the Japanese had become, at least in their formal trade barriers with respect to manufactures, the least protectionist of the advanced capitalist countries."[2]

Some liberalization occurred within domestic institutions. The Administrative Reform Commission, for example, produced a blueprint for a government administration that would be leaner, more streamlined, and better rationalized. The beginning of privatization of public corporations induced more competition and diminished some aspects of bureaucratic control of the economy. The education council stimulated a vigorous debate about the shortcomings of the educational system, but the impetus for reform petered out, and implementation of its recommendations was left to the conservative bureaucrats in the Ministry of Education. Innovations were limited to such items as the introduction of information technology in the curriculum and various internationalization proposals.[3] Progress was made with some of the Maekawa commission recommendations, such as the abolition of the *maruyu* system of incentives for savings and steps to liberalize the financial markets. The distribution system, however, remained an impediment, and changes in the exchange rate were not passed through to the consumer in the form of lower prices. Domestic demand picked up despite rather than because of government policy.

On the global scene, Japan increased its official development assistance to become the world's largest aid donor in 1989 and increased its support of international organizations such as the World Bank, the IMF, and the Asian Development Bank. Japan became "one of the world's largest producers of internationalist rhetoric,"[4] a faithful participant in the GATT negotiations and in the annual economic summit meetings among the economic powers. Yet Japan rarely showed the qualities of leadership and initiative that the new internationalism envisioned. The nation still resisted contributing to the framework of collective security that had protected the open economic order. The vision of changing the structure of the economy to achieve international harmony had barely begun to be implemented. What were the obstacles?

Obstacles to Leadership

Consensus on a new foreign policy is constrained by what we may call, in general, the burdens of history. The legacy of the century-long forced march to catch up with the West has become in the new circumstances a barrier to internationalist consensus. Part of the burden of history is unquestionably institutional, structural, and systemic. To overtake the West, Japan built institutions and political structures that could most efficiently mobilize and allocate resources. The bureaucracy directed the postwar political system into the mid-1970s; it meshed well with business. A strong consensus supported the strategy, laid out in the postwar years by Prime Minister Yoshida, of concentrating on economic recovery while avoiding involvement in international political-strategic affairs. This consensus held firm until the 1970s, when issues of the distribution of the national wealth began to emerge, and foreign criticism and pressures on Japan's industrial policies mounted. Partly for these reasons and partly because of the evolution of political processes, the coherence of bureaucratic leadership weakened and the political system became more complex. Fresh problems split the bureaucracy and spurred infighting among the ministries. Senior LDP politicians who had acquired expertise in policy areas that served special interests made common cause with bureaucrats having jurisdiction over these same areas.

The political scientist Inoguchi Takashi has analyzed this

problem of increasingly powerful triangular relationships that bind "specific vested interests, ministries, and cliques (*zoku*) of Diet members" and in turn block most policy initiatives.

> As a result of this three-way alliance, Japan became a society in which vested interests were virtually inviolable. In such a society government policy initiatives must pass through tortuous channels before their effects can be felt, and the more ambitious the plan is, the more it will be diluted before it can be adopted. . . . Reform efforts evaporate like drops of water on a hot griddle.[5]

Nakatani Iwao, an economist at Osaka University, finds the lack of a strong executive tradition partly responsible for the ponderous decision-making process and the absence of a new sense of national purpose: "The present administration system resembles a massive corporation whose separate divisions are engaged in totally discrete operations and are oblivious to overall corporate goals." He views the fundamental problem, however, as the alliance of bureaucrats, interest groups, and politicians:

> The most problematic Japanese system of all is doubtless the rigid bureaucracy. And one of the biggest problems associated with this system is the activities of politicians aligned with private-sector interest groups who take advantage of it. It is the alliance of bureaucrats, industrial and agricultural interests, and politicians that has closed Japan tight to the rest of the world. Although linkages between specific government agencies and specific industries were effective in many ways during the period of rapid economic growth in the 1960s, they have since acted counter to national interests by intensifying bureaucratic sectionalism. The pace of change has been slowed and international friction intensified by clannish bureaucrats who, with the support of industry-aligned members of the National Diet, have opposed specific reform measures even while endorsing the idea of reform.[6]

Nakasone's grand design of remaking Japan into an international state ran head-on into interest alliances. Initially he excoriated them for obstructing reform. While he was still director of the Administrative Management Agency, he took the unprecedented step of threatening obstinate bureaucrats with penalties and disciplinary measures. Subsequently, as prime minister, he resorted to the appointment of private or ad hoc advisory councils to highlight his ideas, to build popularity, and to evade the intransigence of the bureaucracy. In some cases these strategies were successful, but in other cases they were not. When Nakasone left the prime ministership, he remained dissatisfied with the slow pace of innovation. Leaders of business with dependence on international trade and investment shared his feelings. In the summer of 1988, Gotō Noboru, retired president of the Japanese Chamber of Commerce, wrote that if Japan was to reform itself as an international state, the bureaucracy must be radically restructured.[7]

A veteran high-ranking official of the Ministry of Finance, Sakakibara Eisuke, concludes that the political system is now heavily weighted to the status quo. Bold and aggressive policy departures with more than a one-year time horizon are "quite difficult if not impossible." With "the increasing pluralization and decentralization" of the decision-making process, Sakakibara sees that changing the structure of the socioeconomic system will be "by no means an easy proposition": "Reforming the process will be extremely hard, if not impossible, given that the present decision-making process is the result of a long historical evolution."[8]

In light of the growing strength of the Japanese economy and the consequent self-interest in the maintenance of an open international economy, seemingly, support in Japanese society should be strong enough to overcome bureaucratic infighting, parochial interests, and the immobilism of the political system. Is a free-trade coalition possible? Clearly some groups that are committed to freer trade would favor most of the larger aims of the new internationalism. Komiya Ryūtarō and Itoh Motoshige identify these as leaders of government; the Ministry of International Trade and Industry, except some bureaus in charge of specific industries; the Ministry of Foreign Affairs; parts of the Ministry of Finance; leaders of big business, who are in a position to adopt a national perspective; the Economic Planning Agency; and the Fair Trade Commission. Significantly, Japanese labor has not generally taken a stand against free trade as labor has elsewhere.[9]

Can a free-trade coalition take shape to press the larger agenda of restructuring the economy and in the process transform the Japanese world view? It appears not. Japanese policy making is so highly segmented and policy arenas so self-contained, as Daniel Okimoto argues, that horizontal public interest coalitions emerge only rarely—either in or out of government.[10] A consumer movement, for example, has not been strong enough to overcome the price distortions created by the distribution system. The shallowness of liberalism keeps it from overcoming the many interest groups that resist liberalization and the politicians and bureaucrats who support them. Komiya and Itoh label the Ministries of Agriculture, Public Welfare, Transportation, Post and Telecommunications, and some sections of International Trade and Industry as resisters.[11] Murakami Yasusuké finds the "new middle mass" of Japanese voters still wed to the status quo and unenthusiastic about assuming international responsibilities.[12]

In addition to the systemic handicap of a traditionally weak executive, an unwieldy decision-making process, and immense inroads by parochial interests, any bold policy initiatives prompted by the new internationalism are hobbled by Japan's traditional reactive stance toward the international system. Before the middle of the nineteenth century, Japanese history was almost entirely an indigenous affair; since then, for the most part, Japan has progressed by assessing international conditions and turning them to its own advantage. As a late developer, Japan learned to be responsive to conditions established by the great powers and to react to opportunities that presented themselves. The industrial civilization of the advanced countries provided an image of Japan's future not only in the form of technology but also as models for institutional innovation. Japan's unusual dependence on trade left it, in addition, with a vulnerability that further engendered a cautious and deliberate foreign policy.

As a consequence, since the Meiji Restoration, Japanese leaders have had a keen sensitivity to the forces controlling the international environment; they tried to operate in accord with these forces and use them to their own advantage. A shrewd politician grasped the "trend of the times," adapted Japanese policy to these trends, and benefited from them.

The reactive nature of Japan has been accentuated after World War II. This came about partly from occupation, the status of pariah in the international community, and the nature of the postwar state. The reactive nature in the postwar period also stemmed from the conscious national policy, the so-called Yoshida Doctrine, of focusing on economic growth while the United States guaranteed Japanese security. Economic recovery could be ensured by shrewdly taking advantage of the international order and its exploding free-trade regime. As a vice minister of International Trade and Industry said in 1986, "Japan has usually considered the international economic order as a given condition and looked for ways in which to use it."[13] Otsuka Kazuhiko, director of MITI's Industrial Structure Division in MITI's Industrial Policy

Bureau, concurs with this assessment: "This passive posture has now become so entrenched that the Japanese have a hard time taking action even on economic problems that are largely of their own making—until, that is, they are forced to move by outside pressure."[14]

External Pressure

Outside pressure (*gaiatsu*) is, in fact, another dimension of Japan's reactive stance in international affairs. One of the greatest handicaps to the new internationalism is that Japan has usually not been able to respond institutionally, even in its own best interest, without the intervention of forces outside its system. *Gaiatsu* has become a dynamic of the change, reform, and liberalization that is essential to the agenda of the new internationalism. Inoguchi Takashi, a political scientist who has analyzed the policy problems created by vested interest cliques, sees a necessity for foreign pressure, specifically U.S. pressure, to "transcend the framework of Diet operations, strike down the vested interests syndicate, and remodel Japan into a country committed to a fair society and eager to contribute to the international community."[15]

Strong domestic leadership is an alternative to such pressure, according to Inoguchi: Nakasone was able to disrupt the vested interests cliques. But Tanaka Naoki, assessing the market-opening measures and reforms such as privatization and deregulation of the Nakasone era, sees that "every step was made hand-in-hand, with or under the prodding of, the Reagan administration." Despite his skill at navigating around the power structure to press new policy initiatives, even Nakasone relied on foreign pressure.[16]

U.S. pressure was crucial in easing bureaucratic controls over the Japanese economy, according to the most recent authoritative study of Japanese industrial policy. Only external pressure could have discredited policy tools used in the catch-up period—control of the interest rate structure and the capital market; the use of cartels to limit competition; and other policies regarding trade protection, subsidies, and promotion of technological innovation.[17] Indeed former MITI vice minister Amaya observed that

> it becomes obvious that almost all liberalization policies effected by Japan in the postwar period were implemented due to foreign pressure. Trade liberalization in the early 1960s and capital liberalization in the 1970s, for example, were undertaken reluctantly by industry or the government because of pressure from outside. Financial

111

and communications liberalization in the 1980s, meanwhile, was commenced because of pressure from the U.S.[18]

Where there is no outside pressure, support for the status quo is difficult to dislodge. Nakasone mounted an ambitious program to reform education; while the concept had popular appeal, it was opposed by entrenched bureaucrats in the Ministry of Education and the LDP's education *zoku*. Amaya, a leading advocate of reform on the Education Reform Council, traced its failure to the absence of *gaiatsu*:

> Major reform takes place in Japan only when there is strong pressure from outside. The inside has virtually no initiative—it's all *genjo iji* (support of the status quo). With economics, Japan has been fairly successful since the outside is so strong that it can force reform. But with education there simply is not any outside.[19]

Without a strong national consensus for the new internationalism, the institutional rigidities of the Japanese system allow the reactive nature of the Japanese state to persist. "Japan must not view the 'global community,' " says a 1986 MITI advisory report, "as a society of nations which it can enter at a minimal cost while reaping maximum profit."[20] Nonetheless this remains the prevailing attitude.

The reliance of the internationalists on *gaiatsu* runs the risk of creating a siege mentality in Japan and thereby inflaming a narrow nationalism—another burden of Japanese history. The external pressures for liberalization and for harmonization of Japanese institutions with international norms have created a serious dilemma for Japanese leaders, challenging central features of Japanese culture, social relations, and political structure and arousing nationalist resentment of foreign interference with domestic institutions. Such apparent infringements on Japanese autonomy have rallied xenophobia and ethnocentrism since the beginning of modern Japanese history—and the present is no exception. The young writer Hasegawa Michiko finds *kokusaika* (internationalization) too deferential to Western ways: "*Kokusaika* is a word redolent of the ruthless coercive power to which all non-Western nationals are perforce subject."[21] Similarly, Nishio Kanji, a relentless critic of neoconservatism, writes that Nakasone's advocacy of making Japan an international state amounts to a continuation of postwar deference to U.S. demands.[22] Shimomura Osamu, an architect of the policies and institutions of high growth in the 1960s, wrote a best-selling book, entitled *Japan Is Not at Fault, America Is,* in which he castigated the Maekawa Report for submitting to U.S. views and agreeing to reforms that would deprive the Japanese economy of its strength and vitality: the propensity to save, to work longer hours, and to maintain patterns of work that are culturally sanctioned by Japanese values.[23]

Changing the Culture

The Japanese are perplexed by the issues that are raised by the expectations that its new economic status requires it to adopt a proactive approach to support the international order. *Kokusaika* implies changing Japanese culture in a wide variety of threatening ways: putting foreigners in executive positions of Japanese organizations, admitting foreign labor, accepting women on a more equal basis into social groups, shortening the workweek, changing savings habits, reforming the distribution and sales systems, putting foreign teachers on university faculties, opening research laboratories.

Surveys indicate a deep ambivalence in Japanese attitudes toward *kokusaika*. A 1986 survey by the Economic Planning Agency showed strong support for what we might call superficial internationalization. More than 70 percent of respondents were favorable to increases in "news from abroad," "technology from overseas," "overseas telephone calls and mail," and other categories of information exchange. Similar support existed for short-term human exchanges such as foreign tourists and students. Conversely, for what we might call profound internationalization, such as increases in foreign employees and marriage to foreigners, less than 30 percent approved.[24]

In prewar days the elites used nationalist resentments to mobilize the population for the sacrifices required to catch up with the advanced nations. Now they are chary of an emotional reaction, instead seeing Japan's future interest in accommodation. For Yamazaki Masakazu, Japan has no choice:

> As long as the Japanese economy continues to make its presence felt globally, Japan will find it increasingly difficult to ignore the global community's demands for the internationalization of Japanese culture. Unless Japan is prepared either to conquer the world by force or to stage an economic retreat on all fronts, it has little choice but to accede to these demands.[25]

For Satō Seizaburō, an ardent internationalist, the further advancement of Japan's international position demands such accommodation:

> If we want to attract the world's first class minds to Japan we must resolve to use English. . . . To really strengthen Japan we must open the country to the world. If we stick stubbornly to the Japanese language and Japanese culture the world's superior human talent will simply not come. If we really want to create a *Pax Japonica* in the twenty-first century we must do things like giving our lectures in English. . . . If we don't Japan cannot in the true sense take intellectual leadership in the world.[26]

Similarly, Amaya Naohiro, in a 1987 address to a business group, stressed Japan's self-interest in opening its universities and institutes to foreign researchers: "Repressing nationalism and promoting internationalism will eventually lead to long-term national benefits, particularly in the field of high technology."[27] But Yano Tōru, author of a book on Japanese internationalization, writes that "I see little likelihood of the tightly held nature of the Japanese sense of national identity giving way to an enthusiasm for racial mixing or multinational and ethnic community living." He argues that a cosmopolitan or liberal internationalization is not in the cards, that such internationalization will proceed only as it serves Japan's national interests.[28] This is of course appropriate, but the issue becomes how to define those interests.

From Followership to Leadership

The existence of a liberal international economic order in which norms are established for the free flow of goods and capital based on impersonal market principles is a relatively recent development. It depends on the leadership and self-restraint of the most powerful states in the system. Further, Charles Kindleberger argues, a great power (hegemon) is needed to give stability to such an order and to maintain its norms.[29] Great Britain performed this role in the nineteenth century, and the United States has done so since 1945. They acted not out of idealism or noblesse oblige but rather out of their own long-term self-interest as they perceived it. As Robert Gilpin writes,

> Free trade is the policy of the strong. The conversion of the British from colonialism and formal imperialism to free trade and the Open Door did not reflect a shift in

British ultimate objectives; it represented only a change in methods. The objectives of British policy remained the expansion of British wealth and power.[30]

Nations that are industrial latecomers necessarily have had a different view of their interests. They want to protect themselves from the "imperialism of free trade."[31] Thorstein Veblen argued in *Imperial Germany and the Industrial Revolution* that Germany was the first nation to pursue "a systematic industrial policy and the scientific development of its economy." Japan was not far behind. The lengthy memo on "the encouragement of industry" *(shokusan kōgyō)* that Ōkubo Toshimichi, the strongest of the early Meiji oligarchs, wrote in 1874, showed that he grasped what the German historical school was arguing, namely, "that in a world of free trade the terms of trade tend to favor the most industrially advanced economy, . . . that the British pursued protectionist policies until British industry was strong enough to outcompete every other economy."[32] Itō Hirobumi, who also shaped the politics and economy of the Meiji state and whose attention to the writings of the German historical school is well documented, observed in 1870:

> Now from the lips of Englishmen comes the argument of free trade, and they plot how to introduce it in our country. Since they are really thinking of their own gain, there is great danger to our country from their arguments. Japan should follow the example of the United States and establish a protective tariff to ensure the prosperity of domestic manufactures. When the tariff has outlived its usefulness, then Japan should imitate England and permit free trade.[33]

Like Britain, Japan should adopt a policy of free trade only after its industry has developed behind a shield of protection to where its products could outcompete the products of other economies. The most advanced and efficient economy has no need for tariffs to protect it; instead it requires open markets to sell its superior products and to buy raw materials. "Free trade," Kindleberger remarks, "is the hypocrisy of the export interest, the clever device of the climber who kicks the ladder away when he has attained the summit of greatness."[34]

In the modern world of industrial civilization, in two cases the leading nation has taken responsibility for maintaining an open liberal trading order, sometimes at some short-term cost to itself but ultimately in its own long-term interest. The leader did not at first accept this role. Rather, it was accepted only after protracted struggle between social forces representing the previous economic stage and forces representing the interests of the new wave of industrial innovation. Decades passed before the inertia of the past—the burdens of history—and the resistance to the best interests of the new industrial phase were overcome. In the process, old institutional arrangements had to be put aside, special economic interests representing the previous order were subdued, and interests representative of the leadership of the new wave of industrialism constructed a new liberal institutional framework of global economic order.

In the 1970s the strength and competitiveness of the Japanese economy allowed the nation to remove many formal tariff barriers and also to have a substantial and growing self-interest in the maintenance of the free trade order. In some important advanced industries Japan had not established an advantage and continued the strategy of industrial preemption, denying foreign producers market access until it attained dominance in cost and quality. Nevertheless, the logic of economic strength in many fields and a confident vision of the future were leading the elites to rethink the nation's international role.

The transition from followership to leadership will undoubtedly be a trying process for Japan. Other examples in history of shifting from economic nationalism to liberalism have been so. In England at the close of the Napoleonic Wars, the Tory landholding class used its control of Parliament to pass a new Corn Law and other protective legislation to stem the tide of agricultural imports and the collapse of farm prices and rentals. The gentry and their farmers benefited, but wage earners had to contend with the high price of foodstuffs. A generation of struggle by the Whigs and liberals, representing the new business interests created by industrialization, overcame the mercantilist policies of the Tories. Reform of Parliament in 1832 gave greater representation to the new industrial interests, but not until 1846 were the Corn Laws repealed and Britain entered on its leadership of a liberal international order.

Similarly, the United States struggled for a generation after World War I, when its economic and technological preeminence was established, before shouldering the burden of leadership in restructuring the international economic order. Internationalists like Cordell Hull, arguing that the Great Depression was brought on by mercantilist policies and economic nationalism, revived the Wilsonian vision of an "open and integrated liberal-capitalist world system in which America, with her maturing power and exceptional virtue, would naturally take the leading role."[35] The passage by Congress of the Reciprocal Trade Agreements Act in 1934, which empowered the president to negotiate the reciprocal lowering of tariffs, was a first victory for Hull, but the pressures of export-oriented industries, the need for unimpeded access to raw materials, and the outcome of World War II did not make America's self-interest clear for another decade. The establishment of the IMF-GATT regime marked the victory of internationalism and the commitment to a liberal international order.

The obstacles facing Japan in the transition to a world leader are much more formidable than the previous two cases. An accommodation between its domestic institutions and values and the norms of the liberal international order must be achieved. The internationalists know this will take time, perhaps more time than Japan's trading partners are willing to permit. Moreover, as Amaya has written, Japan lacks two essential qualifications for leadership: an ideology of universal appeal and military power. For the time being, Japan must be content as number two.[36] Kōsaka Masataka similarly has stressed Japan's lack of experience in foreign affairs as an additional reason for maintaining a special relationship with the United States.[37] Murakami Yasusuke likewise agrees that continued U.S. leadership, albeit in modified form, is required. He advocates a "Pax Americana Mark Two" in which America remains preeminent but shares leadership in economic affairs.[38] A June 1988 MITI report, *Nihon no sentaku* (Japan's options), advocates a transition from Pax Americana to a U.S.-centered *Pax Consortis*, in which existing macroeconomic policy coordination among industrialized nations is extended to cooperation in dealing with third world debt, environmental problems,[39] and development assistance.

For the near future, an international division of labor is needed. But for the longer run, Japan must develop a full complement of qualifications for world leadership. No one among Nakasone's partisans expressed this view more eloquently than Amaya, formerly an outspoken proponent of a purely merchant-nation role. By the mid-1980s, convinced of the need for a broader definition of Japanese national interest, he had adopted the internationalist viewpoint. In a 1987 essay entitled "Farewell to the Merchant Nation," Amaya explained that narrow mercantilist pursuits no longer served the national interest. Japan must become what he called a noblesse nation by formulating values and an ideology that would have a universal appeal and thus would

117

qualify the nation for world leadership.[40] Japan must make a conscious choice between following "the path of a merchant nation" and "the path of a noblesse nation":

> At the moment, Japan is somewhere between being a mercantile nation and a true world leader. Our choice is whether to continue the way we are—a strong silver medalist—or go for the gold. Do we have the strength and guts to make it?
>
> As long as Japan remains a merchant-cum-industrialist, we must always defer to the United States. We have to swallow our pride, accept insults and not argue back. Otherwise, we may lose the American market.
>
> If that is too high a price to pay, we have to raise our sights and become a leader. We would need our own ideology, independent defense and economic policies, and leaders who can perform on the world stage.
>
> Shortages of land and resources preclude Japan from ever becoming a classic imperialistic state. But by keeping our government apparatus small and efficient, we can compete with the best.
>
> No matter what Japan decides, the future is fraught with peril. But for me, the choice is clear. Failure in the quest for glory is far more noble than failure in the pursuit of profit.[41]

Between the Past and the Future

In the last decade of the twentieth century, Japan is reminiscent of Janus, the Roman god who is the guardian of portals and the patron of beginnings and endings. He is depicted with two faces, one in front and the other at the back of his head, symbolizing his powers: So with Japan. One face looks forward to the new century: it is fresh, young; its features are still not fully formed. It is a Japan still in the making, preparing for the future, impelled by a robust and sometimes naive optimism; above all, a self-confident Japan, open to the world, assessing new policies, intent on reordering its society and government to meet new challenges. The face of the other Japan is strong, with clear though weather-worn features, looking back over a century-long struggle to achieve world power. It is a Japan still insecure, inward looking, satisfied in its proven ways; a Japan clinging to the order and discipline of its national life, less hospitable to reform, less tolerant of new ways, reluctant to part with the values and institutions that have brought success.

This present period is one of beginnings and endings for Japan. The endings come not from failure but from success; that fact makes change and the development of new policies and institutions enormously difficult. In the aftermath of the Meiji Restoration of 1868 and in the post–World War II period, Japan changed with astonishing rapidity. But these periods of change came in the wake of policy failures, institutional collapse, and national disaster.

The present situation is different. In significant measure the nation has succeeded in achieving the goal with which its modern history began in 1868, namely, to overtake the advanced industrial countries and to establish itself as a world power. This historical goal impelled Japan to build a political-economic structure that would maximize the competitive efficiency of large Japanese manufacturing firms. The effectiveness of this structure, however, now entails mounting political costs abroad as Japan earns large trade surpluses and increasing market shares in other countries, while still maintaining trade-impeding practices against foreign competitors at home.

One of Japan's leading economists, Shimada Haruo, an ardent internationalist, analyzes how Japan's firms are driven to an excessive, unrestrained competition for market share by a commitment to narrow values of microeconomic rationality. This "uncontrolled" competition among companies is the source of Japan's postwar economic vitality, but "with this restricted perspective," Shimada writes, "as the intensity of competition heightens, the race takes on the attributes of an all-out war. Because of this, the boundaries between companies' actions, individual lives, and social norms gradually disappear." Not only does this intense competitive drive dominate national life, it is pursued oblivious to "what represents balance, cooperation, and coexistence in the international community."[42] Rarely in modern history has a nation captured a substantial share of international trade in a short period, and in each case it provoked powerful economic and political reactions in other nations.

A rising international demand for reform of Japan's political-economic structure is sometimes echoed at home, where the all-out drive has been conducted at the expense of the living standard of its own people. In a questionnaire administered by *Nihon keizai shimbun* in March 1990, for example, 86 percent of 10,000 Japanese respondents agreed with the statement that "Japan must take positive measures" in responding to U.S. demands for removal of structural impediments to trade primarily because doing so would help improve their living standard and would be "good for Japan."

Many leaders of Japanese business and government acknowledge the need to change the political-economic structure: Japan must, in its own interests, develop new values and institutions appropriate to the nation's changed international status, a broader definition of national purpose, and a new foreign policy consensus to reflect these changes. Nevertheless, despite this recognition, the new internationalism is still a fragile blossom. Its values, while given lip service, have not been instilled in the lifeblood of the people by their historical and cultural experience. Although they have experienced tutelage in democratic values, they have never on their own achieved a democratic revolution. The Japanese are instinctively more comfortable with collectivist than individualist values, with respect for hierarchy than equality, with productivist than consumerist values, with nationalist sentiment than universalist principles. While these preferences are at once a source of strength in their social cohesion and economic pursuits, they often block smooth relations with other peoples and leadership in the international community. The wartime experience did leave a radical legacy, but Japanese pacifism, coopted by conservative policy makers, has increasingly lost its vitality and taken more the form of isolationism and resistance to an activist world role. Internationalization therefore advances more in reaction to external events rather than to an internally generated sense of national purpose and deeply held values. For the foreseeable future, the principal motive forces of Japanese national life will therefore continue to be the economic dynamism of Japanese firms, the existing political-economic framework within which they operate, the values of economic rationality that support and motivate them, and a reactive adaptation to the political pressures of the international environment.

8

Power and Purpose
in a New Era

Japan made its way in the post-World War II era by relentlessly pursuing its own narrowly defined self-interest and by deliberately frustrating all attempts to engage it in collective security arrangements. This strategy and the underlying foreign policy were a brilliant success because Japan could rely on the United States to guarantee its security and at the same time to maintain the international free trade order, while Japan was free to follow policies of economic nationalism. From time to time Americans complained about the absence of reciprocity in the alliance, but these complaints were always met with rejoinders from the Japanese about their country's pacifism, constitutional constraints, the fears of Japan's neighbors, and the specter of a revived militarism. These assertions of Japan's inability to play a broader role in the international community are now losing much of their persuasive power as a result of changes in the international system. Japan's emergence as an economic power and the end of the cold war have radically changed the context of the alliance. Furthermore, the grudging and limited Japanese contribution to the gulf war coalition once again raised questions about Japan's future national purpose, its policies toward collective security arrangements, and its capacity to change from a country intent solely on its own mercantilist aims to one capable of international leadership.

Largely because of their preoccupation with the cold war, Americans were slow to understand Japan's fundamental national purpose in the postwar period. Essentially Japan has had two coexisting versions of its national purpose since World War II. The popular, public position was based on the imposed constitutional order and its associated reforms and had the support of the articulate opposition groups. According to this version, Japan was rebuilding its national livelihood on the basis of a new democratic order and in line with the role that its constitution envisioned for Japan in the world. The Japanese people had learned the terrible cost of modern warfare. As the first victims of the atomic age, they were convinced that the sovereign prerogative to go to war must be renounced. Japan would lead the world into a new era in which states forswore the settlement of disputes by resort to arms. Japan, in short, had a unique mission and would be an exception to the pattern of all other nations.

This was the face the Japanese showed to the outside world. It was the way a Japanese foreign minister, addressing the United Nations, for example, would explain his country's goals in the world community. Undoubtedly this version of the national purpose appealed to, and was fervently held by, a substantial segment of the Japanese people. It was also the Japanese purpose as it was understood internationally. But clearly this view was sometimes cynically used by the postwar conservative leadership and served as a pretext for their more fundamental and genuine purpose of concentrating exclusively on the goals of economic nationalism. As the former vice minister of the Ministry of International Trade and Industry, Amaya Naohiro, wrote in 1988: "Postwar Japan defined itself as a cultural state holding the principles of liberalism, democracy, and peace, but these were only superficial principles (*tatemae*). The fundamental objective (*honne*) was the pouring of all our strength into economic growth."[1] A genuine pacifism implies willingness to sacrifice for the observance of its principles; cooperating with and taking maximum advantage of U.S. military power, however, called into question Japanese motives. One of Japan's leading social scientists, Murakami Yasusuke, observed in 1990, that

> in a sense the Japanese became a nation of hypocrites, proclaiming adherence to the concept of unarmed neutrality but at the same time quite willing to enjoy the fruits of the economic prosperity made possible by the Pax Americana. The Yoshida doctrine, we might say, ended up sapping the intellectual integrity of Japanese pacifism.[2]

Japan and Collective Security

This primary commitment to economic nationalism also produced a determination to avoid any collective security commitments and any involvement with security affairs beyond the home islands. The 1950 efforts of John Foster Dulles and the State Department to establish a regional security organization like NATO in the Pacific are scarcely remembered today. Dulles proposed to Japan and other countries a Pacific pact, a regional defense alliance, that would facilitate Japanese rearmament but keep it under international control. The pact would initially include the United States, Japan, Australia, New Zealand, the Philippines, and perhaps Indonesia. He believed that such an alliance would internationalize Japanese military forces and "ease reconciliation" with the Japanese constitution.[3] Dulles was prepared to offer guarantees and to override the objections of other Asian countries to secure their acquiescence to Japanese remilitarization and entry into a regional security organization. Such an arrangement, which would have paralleled the contemporary approach to the German question, remains in some form an option today for drawing Japanese defense efforts into a multilateral context and thereby defusing the tensions in the bilateral security treaty. It would encourage a responsible Japanese security commitment and ease concerns of its neighbors of an eventually independent Japanese military.

Prime Minister Yoshida steadfastly refused to participate in such a multilateral Pacific security system. Instead he was determined to use the circumstances of the cold war to Japan's maximum advantage and to pursue a narrowly defined sense of economic self-interest. Yoshida contrived to trade bases on Japanese soil for a U.S. guarantee of Japanese security. It might seem "devious," he confided, but the constitution provided a perfect pretext for resisting U.S. pressure.[4] (The young aide to whom he confided this view was Miyazawa Kiichi, who nearly forty years later, in October 1991, became prime minister himself.)

Avoiding any collective security commitments became an *idée fixe* of postwar Japanese diplomacy. Yoshida and his successors built an elaborate set of policies to prevent Japan's being drawn into any overseas commitments whatsoever. When the Japanese Self-Defense Forces were organized in 1954 because of U.S. pressure, the upper house of the Diet passed a unanimous resolution opposing their overseas dispatch. Subsequent prime ministers held the fixed position that any collective security agreement would be unconstitutional. Other subsequent, complementary policies included the three nonnuclear principles, the three principles proscribing arms and military technology exports, and the limitation of 1 percent of GNP for defense spending. Without these policies and their seemingly incontestable constitutional sanction, the pressure on Japan to contribute to the cold war effort would have been well-nigh irresistible. As Sonoda Sunao, who served as foreign minister in 1977–1978, recalled: "The Americans were always asking us to do this and do that, to take over part of the burden of their Far Eastern policies. But all their efforts were sabotaged by one Japanese cabinet after another."[5] The U.S. preoccupation with the cold war, observed the conservative writer Nishio Kanji, allowed Japan "to conduct a diplomacy that exploited and totally used the United States. Even if Japan was asked to take some responsibility, we could get away with avoiding it and simply pursue our own economic interests."[6] Kōsaka Masataka, a frequent LDP adviser, said that the elite strategy was that "Japan should only increase its defense capability just enough so as not to worsen the U.S.-Japan relationship, since the nation's security depends on a favorable mood in this relationship."[7]

President George Bush told Prime Minister Kaifu Toshiki at their California summit meeting in April 1991, following the Persian Gulf War, that he hoped "most Americans understand the constitutional constraints on Japan."[8] Clearly, however, the constitution, particularly Article 9, has often been cynically used and interpreted by the mainstream conservative leadership to suit their political needs and their fundamental, though rarely articulated, definition of Japanese national purpose. Their interpretations of the constitution as prohibiting collective security commitments have been political rather than legal judgments. As the *Sankei shimbun,* a leading conservative newspaper, wrote in an editorial on September 12, 1990, during the controversy over Japanese participation in the multilateral force in the Persian Gulf: "The national charter does not specifically ban such a sovereign right. . . . We think it is silly to bind our own hands with such an interpretation that reflects self-serving political considerations of government leaders."

Minimalist interpretations of what the constitution permits have been offered to avoid being drawn into collective security arrangements and to avoid the domestic controversy and disruption that would attend a more active foreign policy. We now know that the U.S. and Japanese drafters of the constitution explicitly intended that Article 9 should not be interpreted to conflict with Article 43 of the UN Charter, which requires all UN members to make available to the Security Council "on its call . . . armed forces . . . for the purpose of maintaining international peace and security." At the time the draft of the constitution was being discussed and prior to its approval, Yoshida and other conservatives expressed concern that Article 9 might complicate Japan's future membership in the United Nations. Charles Kades, the U.S. colonel in the government section of the occupation who was responsible for drafting the constitution, maintained, however, that "the Ashida amendment appeared intended to alleviate their concerns; and it certainly was not an objective of the Occupation to put any obstacle in the way of Japan becoming a full-fledged member of the United Nations."[9] Subsequent interpretations of the constitution as constraining Japan from participating in UN peace-keeping operations did not represent the intentions of the drafters.

The growth of Japanese power, the end of the cold war, and Japan's limited commitment to the gulf coalition have made an issue of the minimalist interpretations of Article 9. In the midst of the gulf crisis, Inoki Masamichi, the moderate, scholarly, and widely respected former head of the National Defense Academy and now head of a research institution on security problems, observed that when Japan wanted to maintain a low posture in international politics and to avoid doing things expected of it by the international community, it frequently resorted to what he called "the devious (zurui) measure of using the Constitution as a pretext." In uncharacteristically strong language, he condemned it as "a despicable way of escaping responsibility" (kitanai nigeguchi). Inoki, who does not favor constitutional revision, argues that Self-Defense Forces should participate in UN peace-keeping forces: under the constitution, Japan possesses the full right of participating in collective security arrangements. This was implied in joining the United Nations in 1956.[10]

The belated decision in April 1991, in response to intense international criticism of its inadequate support of the gulf coalition, to send minesweepers to the gulf demonstrates the arbitrary way in which the constitution has been reinterpreted. Only three years earlier, during the 1987 gulf crisis, the government equivocated and finally refused to dispatch minesweepers. At that time Prime Minister Nakasone created a stir by declaring in the Diet that sending minesweepers to the gulf did not contravene the constitution. Faced with opposition within his own administration and with his term in office running out, he did not press the issue.

The advantage of maintaining a low posture in international affairs since World War II has been the ability not only to concentrate exclusively on economic growth but also to avoid the extreme internal political divisions that an active foreign policy would have engendered. For most of the postwar period, the conservative mainstream and the left-wing progressive camp tacitly agreed to avoid the divisive issues of rearmament and constitutional revision. Avoiding collective security commitments has had the great advantage not only of limiting defense spending but of enhancing domestic political stability. Japan alone among advanced industrial nations has been shielded from the social stresses of an active foreign policy.

Conversely, the cost of this low-posture policy is becoming increasingly clear. The Yoshida Doctrine took on a life of its own. It began as a strategy for handling the international politics of the cold war and the domestic politics of pacifism. But as the years of its success lengthened, many of the institutions and processes required for an active and independent foreign policy were left undeveloped. While the Ministry of Finance, the Ministry of International Trade and Industry, the Economic Planning Agency, and, on some issues, big business dominated the formulation of foreign policy, the growth of institutions of autonomous policy making in the security field was stunted. Institutions of intelligence gathering, strategic thinking, crisis management, policy implementation, and, of course, the armed forces went undeveloped. The commonly heard assertion that Japan has the world's third or fourth largest defense budget gives a wholly mistaken impression, overlooking as it does the dramatic change in the exchange rate, the high cost of weapons development in Japan, the high cost of personnel and land rent, the substantial sums that pay the expenses of the American bases, and other peculiarities of the Japanese defense budget.

But a more costly and basic result of the moratorium that Japan has enjoyed is the state of internal Japanese opinion. As a result of the Yoshida strategy, the conservatives have abnegated the responsibilities of the leadership in a democracy to inform and to educate its citizenry. The debate over the role in the Persian Gulf demonstrated the divisions, the parochialism, and isolationism that sway Japanese views, even among the elite. The opposition to a more positive foreign policy, that is, toward acceptance of collective security commitments, is less ideological today than in the past. The Socialist party, once the stout defender of unarmed neutralism, after a brief resurgence in the aftermath of the Recruit scandal in 1988–1989, has resumed its steady decline. Instead opposition to the government's wholly innocuous United Nations Peace Cooperation Bill in the autumn of 1990, which would have permitted dispatch of personnel to the gulf, came from a mixture of complacency, anti-American nationalism, and residual distrust of a situation in which the postwar restraints on an expanded military would be removed. Decades of shunning collective security arrangements, of accommodating left-wing opinion, and of minimalist interpretations of their constitution have left Japanese opinion adrift and reactive in its attitudes toward post–cold war foreign policy.

Japan and the Gulf War

Politics in Japan was thrown into turmoil by the first major international crisis of the post–cold war era. Debate over Japanese participation in the gulf coalition quickly turned into the theater of the absurd and created a classic case of immobilism in the Japanese political system. Foreign policy issues that had been pointedly and purposefully evaded for decades as a means of maintaining domestic political consensus now had to be confronted and new policies devised if Japan was to respond in a way befitting its new self-confidence. Most fundamental was the issue of collective security. Opposition party and mainline conservative politicians generally argued that the constitution prohibited the dispatch of Self-Defense Forces abroad. Prime Minister Kaifu was disposed to agree, but under pressure from an alliance of political nationalists and internationalists in his party who wanted to dispatch SDF personnel to join the coalition, he waffled and proposed the United Nations Peace Cooperation Bill. The compromise pleased almost no one and wholly evaded the issue of collective security. Rather than assert the need, under changed international circumstances, for a new constitutional interpretation, Kaifu continued the politics of pretense.

The bill proposed the establishment of a UN Peace Cooperation Corps (UNPCC), in which SDF members could hold joint status and which could assist in UN peace-keeping operations as long as they did not entail the use of force. UNPCC members could carry small arms for personal safety, and they could assist in rearguard support activities of the multinational force; the UNPCC would report directly to the prime minister to ensure civilian control.

The hastily drafted bill was debated in a special session of the Diet. Discussion concentrated almost wholly on its constitutionality with little attention accorded to the significance of the international crisis and Japanese responsibility in light of its dependence on the gulf for 70 percent of its oil supply. In the face of strident opposition in the Diet and the bill's unpopularity in opinion polls, it was withdrawn after twenty-two days of heated debate. Underlying much of the constitutional controversy was what we have called the Japanese question, that is, the lack of trust in civilian controls over the military and a continuing fear even among the Japanese themselves that Japan's character as a nation still harbored the potential for oppression at home and aggression abroad.

Other Japanese efforts to support the coalition proved an even more shameful spectacle of disarray. Initially a medical team of 100 specialists was promised, but less than twenty volunteers could be found. After a brief stint in the region, even they returned home. Tokyo also pledged that Japanese civilian aircraft and ships would transport food, water, and medical supplies, but airlines and longshoremen recoiled from involvement in the hostilities, and the pledge was never fulfilled.

Nor was the usual response of a merchant nation of providing financial assistance handled any more adroitly. Initially a government spokesman said that Japan would not act as "a cash dispensing machine," but under U.S. pressure, a $1 billion contribution was grudgingly offered. The Foreign Ministry announced that under no circumstances, even if war broke out, could this amount be increased. In anger the U.S. House of Representatives voted overwhelmingly to begin withdrawing 5,000 troops a year from Japan unless Japan agreed to pay all costs of keeping U.S. troops there. Within forty-eight hours the Japanese government announced an additional $3 billion contribution to the gulf coalition. Subsequently, when war broke out and Tokyo still lacked contingency plans for providing any other kind of assistance, the government pledged an additional $9 billion.

The debate ended as it began—in confusion and disarray. By avoiding the fundamental issue of collective security, Kaifu failed to lead public thinking and to focus the debate on the need for a historic change of course. The *Yomiuri*, a leading newspaper, editorialized:

> In order to meet the challenge we face, it is urgent that we re-evaluate the constitutional interpretations that have been accumulated throughout the Cold War era and establish a new route to peace based on a new perspective in the days of the "post–Cold War." For example, there is the interpretation that the collective right of self-defense is unconstitutional, but there is no express stipulation to that effect in the constitution. It is merely the interpretation of successive cabinets, formulated within the framework of the Cold War.[11]

Reflecting on the shambles of Japan's international position after the utter failure to formulate policies during the gulf war, former prime minister Nakasone traced the cause back to Yoshida's handling of defense policy in the 1950s and the "irresponsible" course on which it set Japanese policy and opinion. In a long and sober dialogue with Kōsaka Masataka, published in May 1991, Nakasone observed that

> in my view, Yoshida at that time should have said [to the Japanese people] that even though Japan is impoverished it is wrong if a people do not defend their own country; it will not do to continue this way; and once we recover our economic capability we must have commensurate military power in order to carry out our international responsibilities. Yoshida bears a heavy responsibility for his failure to say these things. . . . Thus when I became prime minister, I said "we must extricate ourselves from the Yoshida system."[12]

Kishi Nobusuke had tried to correct the Yoshida policy, Nakasone went on, but by the time he was prime minister, public opinion had become blindly committed to pacifism as the best way to preserve their livelihood. Ikeda Hayato subsequently determined to practice "patience and forbearance" on all controversial security issues, and Satō Eisaku too found this course to be the easiest and most comfortable for a politician. As a consequence, according to Nakasone, the Japanese people were sheltered from the reality of international politics; the debate on the gulf war turned on superficial issues of how much money was sufficient to contribute, whether the Self-Defense Forces should be dispatched, and what they should be permitted to do. What was necessary was "to return to the fundamental issues of Yoshida's day"—namely, the question of what constituted the fundamental obligations of a nation-state—which had been wrongly decided. Strong leadership, Nakasone concluded, was required to reeducate the Japanese people and to wean them from the politics of "prevarication" (gomakashi), "escapism" (tohishugi), and "ostrich-like pacifism."

Despite the prevailing nationalist mood in Japan, the mainstream elites continue to hold to a consensus in favor of reliance on the U.S. security guarantee. In the early postwar period, these policies were a short-term means to Japanese political and economic recovery, but by the 1970s, these elites had become convinced that as a consequence of the nuclear stalemate, the struggle for power in the international system was shifting to the economic realm and that large military establishments would only prove a burden in the intensifying global economic competition. They were convinced, in short, that Japanese security depended on its economic strength.

Of the mainstream LDP leaders, no one better epitomizes today the resolute adherence to the Yoshida Doctrine and the view that Japan must remain an exception to the normal pattern of nation-states than Prime Minister Miyazawa Kiichi, formerly foreign minister and minister of finance. Miyazawa, who as a young man was an aide to Yoshida, has tenaciously defended a passive international role of Japan by pointing out that the constitution makes Japan a "special state" (tokushu kokka) and precludes it from normal participation in international politics.

In creating a "peace state," Miyazawa wrote in 1984, "the Japanese people (minzoku) have gambled their future (unmei) in a great experiment, the first of its kind in human history." Accordingly, Japan cannot justify any point of view other than its own self-interest. Japan's foreign policy, Miyazawa told an interviewer in 1980, "precludes all value judgments. It is a pretense of a foreign policy. The only value judgments we can make are determining what is in Japan's interest. Since there are no real value judgments possible we cannot say anything." When challenged politically, Japan can only defer. "All we can do when we are hit on the head is pull back. We watch the world situation and follow the trends." This reactive stance was illustrated when the Japanese government dealt with the gulf crisis. Miyazawa stoutly opposed sending Self-Defense Forces or even providing logistical help such as transportation and communications. Medical assistance under UN auspices was as far as he would go. "We must clearly state that we cannot change the Japanese Constitution at this time. Even if other countries say that having such a constitution is outrageous (keshikaran) we must maintain the position that we decided on this and it's not for others to interfere."[13]

In the fall of 1991, after assuming the prime ministership, Miyazawa, acceding to international criticism and pressure and to the demands of the Takeshita faction, to which he owed his election, gave his support to legislation that authorized dispatch of Self-Defense Forces abroad to participate in UN peace-keeping operations. The legislation set five conditions for participation: a cease-fire agreement must exist; a Japanese role must be accepted by parties directly involved in conflicts; a UN force must be neutral; the Self-Defense Forces must be withdrawn once a truce collapses; and the personnel would be allowed to use arms only in self-defense. Blithely altering his long-held position, Miyazawa said the dispatch of Self-Defense Forces overseas would not be unconstitutional because they would have no intention of using force. His altered stance was the quintessence of the Yoshida strategy: it offered a pragmatic, minimalist concession in response to strong foreign pressure.

The Japanese Role in Asia

The gulf crisis demonstrated once again that Japan's capacity to change, to develop policies that transcend its own narrow self-interest, and to play a role of international leadership in a way that would satisfy world expectations is severely limited by the institutional legacies of the postwar experience. Nevertheless, one emerging role of leadership follows almost naturally from the trajectory of the postwar Japanese state: to lead Asia's emergence as the world's most dynamic economic region. This role is developing almost ineluctably from the needs of the Japanese economy, from international political-economic trends, and from the predilections of Japan's dominant postwar institutions and their bureaucratic and business leadership. The implications of this development for the United States and the international system are substantial.

Since 1985, Japan has acquired an impressive array of economic tools that make it possible to establish economic leadership in the region. A remarkable convergence of developments in the mid-1980s provided the opportunity for Japan's emergence as the core economy of an increasingly cohesive and interdependent region. These developments included the Plaza Hotel Accord of 1985 and the rise in the value of the yen, Japan's emergence as the world's largest creditor and donor of official development assistance (ODA), liberalization of the Japanese capital market, and foreign pressure to restructure the Japanese economy so as to reduce its trade surpluses and to increase the import of manufactured goods. As a consequence of these developments, Japan was prepared to offer other Asian countries a persuasive set of economic inducements to follow its leadership: foreign aid, commercial loans, technology transfer, direct investment, and preferential access to the Japanese market.

As a result, Japan provided leadership to Asia's development as a more cohesive and interdependent region. In the latter half of the 1980s, intra-Asian trade and investment expanded remarkably. Intraregional East Asian trade began to exceed trans-Pacific flows in the late 1980s. Total trade (exports plus imports) among the fifteen major Asian economies grew 30 percent in 1987 and 31 percent the following year, by which time Asia's exports to other Asian countries exceeded Asia's exports to North America. Japan played the leading role in this remarkable development. Exports from Asian countries to Japan sharply increased in 1988: Thailand (53 percent), Hong Kong (50 percent), Korea (42 percent), Philippines (44 percent), and Singapore (31 percent).[14] Similarly, Japan was the driving force in intra-Asian investment. In 1987 and 1988, Japanese investment in Asia grew 73 percent and 45 percent, respectively.

In the late 1980s, Japanese bureaucrats began to devote their attention to the disposition of these sources of economic influence within the region. The task of formulating a comprehensive and coordinated approach to Asia in terms of economic policies fit the postwar inclination of the Japanese state, with its strength in economic institutions, capacity for bureaucratic planning and coordination, and ability to fine-tune policies to enhance market forces. Given Japan's reservoir of private capital for investment, its commitment to provide massive official aid, and its stores of transferable technologies, the bureaucrats could use a mix of government and private resources to promote Japanese influence and power. Concern that rising protectionism and development of trading blocs would restrict that access to Europe and North America further focused their attention on Asia.

Speaking in Bangkok in June 1991, Miyazawa Kiichi said that Japan should lead an Asian economic bloc that included South Korea and the Association of Southeast Asian Nations: that is, Japan should use its economic resources to build the region's economic infrastructure for the long term and to help this bloc "outdo" the North American and European blocs. "The Asian economic zone," he said, "will outdo the North American economic zone and European economic zone at the beginning of the twenty-first century and assume a very crucial role."[15] Economic complementarities, geographic proximity, and cultural traditions all enhance the attractiveness of the proposed Japanese role in Asia.

In the late 1980s, the Ministry of Finance, the Ministry of International Trade and Industry, the Economic Planning Agency, and the Ministry of Foreign Affairs undertook major studies to examine Japan's relations within the region and the ways in which Japan might promote the region's economic integration. A 1988

EPA study recommended a comprehensive integration of the economies of Asia with the Japanese bureaucracy serving as the "Asian brain" that would mastermind the region's economy, determining its development through investment and technology.[16]

In 1987, MITI announced its New Asian Industries Development Plan, or New AID Plan, designed to relocate Japanese industry into lower-cost Asian countries, which was happening anyway because of ineluctable economic forces. This New AID Plan gave MITI a tool to guide the market forces and thereby to assert its influence over the process of restructuring the economy, easing trade frictions, and promoting commercial advantage. Private investment, trade, and ODA should be coordinated so they served as a "trinity" or "three sides of one body *(sanmi-ittai)*."[17] In 1990, an *Asian Wall Street Journal* correspondent was shown MITI's elaborate and detailed study designed to make Malaysia a leader in word processors, answering machines, and facsimile devices. A MITI section chief showed him an array of blueprints drafted with Malaysian planners for industries ranging from sports shoes to color television picture tubes.[18]

Given the long experience of Japanese bureaucrats in creating institutions and formulating policies to promote Japan's own economy, what is likely to emerge is a series of policies to direct the regional division of labor under quiet Japanese leadership. These various policies seek a Japanese-style economic leadership that advances the cause of Japan's domestic restructuring and improves its trade imbalance with the United States at the same time that it lays the basis for a soft, regionwide integration of economies under Japanese leadership. Japan's policies do not envision a closed economic bloc that would formally limit free trade and the ability of other countries to trade in the region. Japan's emerging advantages are so substantial that such restrictions would not be required. Instead the policies envision a de facto bloc.

The "soft" and "quiet" nature that Japan's leadership in the Asia-Pacific region would adopt is suggested by the conclusions emerging from an ambitious study recently undertaken by the Ministry of Finance. The study bore the imprint of Nagatomi Yūichirō, the most able organizer of bureaucratic thinking in the Japanese government. A decade earlier he had directed the Ōhira Research Groups. With prime ministerial backing, Nagatomi and his colleagues in MOF in 1988 set up the Committee for Asia-Pacific Economic Research composed of leading figures from academia, business, and government, many of whom had served earlier on the Ōhira commissions. Drawing explicitly on the internationalism of the Ōhira studies, the committee's interim report, issued in 1990, rejected the economic nationalism of the postwar era: "The future Japan cannot, and must not, exist within the closed narrow vision of prosperity and safety only for itself." Instead it was necessary to open markets, to expand domestic demand, and to encourage interdependence. Above all, the report rejected political nationalism. Japan "learning the lessons of history" would remain a "non-military economic power," a "non-ideological nation," and a "new-style peace-loving and cultural nation."[19]

Sophisticated cultural policies could facilitate the emerging Japanese leadership role in Asia. The report recommended the dissemination and teaching of Japanese culture and the construction of

> a vast comprehensive museum of Japanese history, and a museum of contemporary Japan, a so-called "Japanese Smithsonian Museum area" . . . to convey to the peoples of the Asia-Pacific region Japan's historical experiences . . . , clarifying the formation process of the Japanese poly-civilization, which was fostered through international exchange with the various regions of the world including the Asia-Pacific region.[20]

It recommended establishment of Japanese cultural centers in the key cities of the Asia-Pacific region, promotion of cultural exchanges, and organization of hospitality centers in all Japanese cities for Asia-Pacific students studying there.

Such bureaucratic thinking envisions a kind of "benign division of labor" coordinated and presided over by Japan.[21] The favorite metaphor for this pattern of development is the "flying geese" formation, a phrase coined by Akamatsu Kaname, a prewar Japanese economist, but more recently popularized by former foreign minister Ōkita Saburō. This pattern of regional development prescribes a lead economy with others ranked behind in the order of their economic strength and technical sophistication. This analogy suggests a vertical division of labor, not wholly unlike what was envisioned in Japan's prewar pan-Asian ideology. The report of MOF's Committee on Asia-Pacific Economic Research, for example, foresees a three-tier division of labor in Asia composed of: (1) Japan, (2) the newly industrializing economies (NIEs), that is, South Korea, Hong Kong, Taiwan, and Singapore, and (3) the ASEAN countries and China. While denying that this would be a fixed structure, the report seems to minimize the possibility of changing the order of countries when it describes future development in the region:

> While each area continues to develop, a new international division of labor will be formed in a far higher dimension than in the past. . . .
>
> For the development of each of the three tiers, it is necessary that what Japan used to do should be done by the Asian NIEs, what the Asian NIEs used to do should be done by ASEAN countries, and Japan should enter into a far higher division. For this, it is indispensable for Japan to encourage maturer industries to make inroads abroad positively.[22]

Under Japanese leadership, the countries of Asia would move successively up the ladder of the product cycle.

Aid is a powerful instrument for Tokyo bureaucrats to wield in planning the coordination of Asian economies. The new MOF vice minister for international affairs, Chino Tadao, declared in August 1991 that he would bend all his efforts toward transforming Japanese official development assistance into a magnet for private capital, using it as "seed money to attract Japanese manufacturers" with an attractive investment environment.[23] U.S. aid has been used to create markets, but the distinction of the emerging Japanese ODA program is its more highly coordinated and guided nature and its more unmitigatedly commercial purpose. Turf battles do exist, however, among the bureaucrats who formulate policy. (No Diet legislation has established formal policy guidelines for Japanese ODA.)[24] The Foreign Ministry, MOF, and MITI all contend for influence. MOF is concerned about cost-effectiveness; the Foreign Ministry is more concerned about diplomatic objectives; MITI looks to commercial advantage. In line with MITI's "internationalist" outlook, its conception of Japan's national interest is now broader. Instead of attention to single, closely tied infrastructure projects—a dam, a harbor development, or a highway—the strategy of the Japanese government is now more proactive and comprehensive, more attentive to the development of structural complementarities with the Japanese economy.[25]

The methodical and meticulous way in which the New AID Plan is implemented typifies the new approach. It moves through three stages. First, an economic master plan is developed for a target country to identify industries that would be internationally competitive, susceptible to Japanese leadership, and appropriate to a vertical integration. The Ministry of Foreign Affairs officials then approach the government of the recipient country and engage them in a dialogue about Japanese assistance in a comprehensive plan for its industrialization. Second, assuming the government is receptive to Japanese investment and leadership, a set of specific guidelines for the appropriate industries is worked out, detailing what changes and incentives must be accomplished to justify official Japanese support and private investment. Third, a host of official Japanese aid institutions is brought into play to implement a program of construction and investment.[26]

The importance of defining Japan's national interest more broadly, as advocated by the new internationalists, is nowhere clearer than in implementing Japan's new Asian strategy. The effort to influence the development of Asian economies through the coordinated use of trade, aid, private investment, and technology transfer requires all the sensitivity and finesse that Tokyo can muster. Suspicion and resentment of Japan in Asia, which are the legacy of the world war, leave no room for the self-confident bombast of the political nationalists or the narrowly self-interested methods of economic nationalism. Sophisticated leaders of the bureaucracy and big business recognize that a more accommodative approach and a broader sense of the national interest is required. The kind of precautions prescribed by MITI's 1986 study, *Japan in the World*—for example, accommodation of Japanese business practice to the local culture, promotion of host country managers, transfer of significant technology to the host country, philanthropic activities, and care to ensure that host countries share substantially in the economic benefits of Japanese investment—are essential.

Japan and the United States in Asia

The new Japanese role in Asia increases the problems of the Japanese-U.S. alliance; it especially challenges the willingness of the United States to continue providing security for the region while it cedes economic leadership to the Japanese. In the past the United States exercised unchallenged leadership in the Pacific Basin. Through its support of international institutions such as the World Bank and GATT, it created a favorable environment in which the economies of this region could flourish. It encouraged the success of the export-led strategies by absorbing huge volumes of imported manufactures. Through its military power it maintained the political and security dimensions of the region. The U.S. government provided aid, and multinationals made direct investments in the region. Technology was transferred: American universities trained large numbers of Asians in science and engineering.

Thailand is the most dramatic example of how leadership roles have changed. From 1970 to 1985, U.S. investment in Thailand was slightly higher than Japanese, but in the years since, Japan's share has increased and now outstrips the U.S. share. The Japanese ambassador to Bangkok, Okazaki Hisahiko, estimated in 1991 that "a new Japanese factory will open in Thailand every three days for the next several years." Japanese economic aid to Thailand in 1991 ran an estimated $500 million, while the United States provided less than $20 million.[27]

As Japanese economic power in Asia becomes marked, Americans will confront in a stark way the need for a coherent policy of their own that integrates new strategic and economic realities. It appears that the U.S. security system will be keeping order for an economically and technologically thriving region dominated by Japan. Such an arrangement is of questionable stability. Although U.S. forces have been in Japan not only for the defense of Japan but also to serve American interests, American opinion is unlikely to continue support for the maintenance of more than 40,000 military personnel in Japan, even though under an agreement signed in 1991 the Japanese government will by 1995 assume approximately half the cost of keeping U.S. bases and forces in Japan. Americans are not likely to accept indefinitely a role akin to mercenaries.

Left to their own wishes in Asia, Japanese policy makers would have the Americans continue to carry the burdens of their security. As the Japanese political analyst Inoguchi Takashi observed recently, Japan "is concerned about the United States declining too early and too fast. . . . It is clearly not in the interest of Japan to see the United States prematurely decline."[28] Although American decline is presumed, its leadership is still needed. This dependence on the alliance implies resentment over the continued deference to U.S. political leadership, but Japan grudgingly pays that price.

As mentioned in chapter 2, the March 1990 remarks of the top Marine Corps general in Japan caused intense private anger among Japanese. He told a *Washington Post* correspondent that U.S. troops must remain in Japan at least until the beginning of the twenty-first century because "no one wants a rearmed, resurgent Japan. So we are a cap in the bottle, if you will." The resentment this statement caused at a time when Japan was being pressed to pay more of the costs of U.S. bases is understandable.

An incident, in April 1990, also implied that a future purpose of the Mutal Security Treaty was containment of Japanese rearmament. A high-profile Pentagon report, "A Strategic Framework for the Asian Pacific Rim: Looking toward the Twenty-first Century," listed a key strategic U.S. objective in Japan as "discouraging any destabilizing development of power projection capability." An anonymous senior Defense Department official explained that the United States did not want to see Japanese aircraft carriers deployed in the Indian Ocean. These incidents stirred understandable resentment within the Japanese diplomatic and defense establishment. A *Yomiuri shimbun* columnist wrote in late March 1990 that at a time when Congress and the Bush administration were demanding that Japan increase its support from 40 percent to 100 percent of the appropriate yen-based expenses of maintaining U.S. bases in Japan, the notion that these forces were intended to contain Japanese rearmament was, at the least, offensive. "Some Japanese cannot feel good about paying for a watchdog that watches them," the columnist concluded. Significantly, however, when Japanese policy makers discussed these incidents, they suppressed their anger in deference to Japan's larger interest of keeping the U.S. military in Asia and maintaining the stability of the region.

These incidents not only reveal the changing tone of the bilateral relationship, they raise the larger issue of Japanese-U.S. relations in Asia in the post–cold war era. To assign the Mutual Security Treaty the purpose of containing Japanese power and influence in the Pacific does not square with the prevailing nationalist mood in Japan. Ishihara Shintarō's reaction in 1989 to such an arrangement was characteristically inflammatory while nonetheless pointing to the larger issue:

> Japan's franchise is Asia. I think Japan should assume greater responsibility than the U.S. or Europe in the development of the Asian region. It is extremely unpleasant to watch the U.S. drive a wedge between Japan and other Asian countries by propagating the idea that the U.S. military presence is preventing Japan's invasion of the region. In combining the human capital of the Newly Industrialized Countries of Asia with Japan's high technology and knowledge-intensive industry, Asia could become a powerful economic bloc.[29]

The day is likely to arrive when Japan will reject the anomaly of financing foreign bases that are largely designed to contain Japan, particularly when this situation contributes to a politically deferential and dependent foreign policy.

Probably no more widely held view exists in Japan regarding its future international role than the belief that technology and industry are the basis of national power in the contemporary world and that America's declining and Japan's increasing industrial strengths are creating a new balance of power that should be reflected in a new Japanese assertiveness. This is expressed not only in the chauvinism of an Ishihara Shintarō but by a growing number of bureaucrats and politicians. It is also expressed by influential intellectuals like Murakami Yasusuke, who wrote in 1988:

> The very ideals sustaining modern Western society are being shaken. . . . The Japanese challenge [is] a development of global historical significance. Japan has had even greater success than the United States in building an advanced mass society. At least from an institutional viewpoint, Japan has probably outdone Western Europe and North America in the guarantee of liberties. . . . Japan has also achieved greater equality than almost any country in the West. Most important, the secret of Japan's success relates at least in part to non-Western organizational principles. Furthermore, the same phenomenon is occurring in Hong Kong, Singapore, South Korea, and Taiwan; what we seem to be witnessing is not simply a Japanese challenge but an Asian challenge, a development that cannot but call into question the very basis of the Pax Americana.[30]

A wide spectrum in Japan is experiencing an increasing impatience with a deferential and dependent foreign policy and a growing will to exert leadership in the region, even while there is no agreement on quite how this should be done.

A New Era

Asia is on the verge of a new era. The resurgence of Japan, the new economic vitality of the region, and the end of the cold war are driving Asia toward a third great transformation of its organizing structure of regional politics in this century.[31] Both of the previous transformations came at the end of wars; both were achieved through American leadership; and both shaped the fundamental nature of U.S.-Japanese relations for the succeeding decades. American leadership is needed again to respond to the changes created by the end of the cold war and to establish a new structure and motivating spirit of Asian politics to fit the new conditions in the region.

The first transformation, which came about after the destruction by World War I of the imperialist balance of power in East Asia, was an attempt to reorganize the region on the basis of Wilsonian principles. At the Washington Conference of 1921–1922, the Americans insisted on termination of the Anglo-Japanese alliance and its replacement by vague multilateral treaties upholding the open door in China and based on a vision of a liberal capitalist world order, evolving through peaceful economic competition and interdependence. The Washington system did not enhance international security because the Americans, after establishing the system, failed to support it, much less to give it leadership. The Japanese were never fully assimilated into the new order. Powerful domestic forces opposed it as contrary to Japan's national aspirations, and they rather easily outflanked the internationalists, who wanted to cooperate with the Western powers. Yoshida Shigeru, who had been a member of the Japanese delegation at Versailles in 1919, idealized the Anglo-Japanese alliance and believed its termination was a blunder for all concerned that deprived Japanese diplomacy of its firm footing and set Japan on the path to militarism. "Without the stabilizing influence of the Alliance," he later wrote, "our military men saw fit to overrun Manchuria and China; the Second World War started, which was a blow to Britain and reduced China to chaos; and everyone knows what happened to us."[32]

The second great structural transformation of international relations in the Pacific followed World War II with the establishment of the Pax Americana, the organization of a system of collective security arrangements to contain Communist expansion, and massive aid and development programs designed to stabilize the region and to promote democratic politics. The American-devised institutional framework was an astonishing success in transforming Asia from a "war ravaged, largely post-colonial international backwater into the most rapidly expanding economic region in the world."[33]

Japan's postwar order, including both its domestic political economy and its international role, was shaped by the special relationship with the United States. Yoshida regarded an alliance with the United States as a replacement for the Anglo-Japanese alliance, for he believed that Japan's destiny was "to be a global power, and that the expansion as well as security of the state was best guaranteed by close alliance with the dominant Western power in Asia and the Pacific."[34] Because of the unique circumstances in which it was formed, that is, during the occupation of Japan, the U.S.-Japan alliance was wholly different from its predecessor. It was an unequal, nonreciprocal alliance. American hegemony in the postwar world, and particularly its hegemony over Japan, was so unprecedentedly great that it has proved difficult for both sides to come to terms with a much more equal and reciprocal relationship, such as would exist in a normal alliance. The extraordinary rise of Japan as an economic superpower is, to a considerable extent, the result of this special relationship; the mainstream of the LDP is committed to its continuation for the time being in more or less its present form. Japan likewise was essential to U.S. postwar global strategy, and although perplexed by the economic competition of the Japanese, U.S. policy makers are, in the absence of an alternative vision of a new foreign policy, generally reluctant to undertake substantial changes, preferring instead gradual, incremental adjustments. For much of the postwar period the special relationship was comfortable to both the Americans and the Japanese. Americans welcomed Japanese *deference* and Japanese welcomed *dependence* on the United States. It is not easy to abandon so comfortable a relationship.

Nonetheless, the end of the cold war, the dramatic change in the relative economic strength of Japan and the United States, and the vitality of the region have vitiated the original purposes of the alliance. At the same time, the alliance in its present form is the subject of a growing opposition in the United States that is reflected in the media and in Congress. In Japan it is the subject of a visceral nationalist opposition that continues to mount. The anomalies in the alliance as it is are unsustainable in the new conditions. U.S. interests require the establishment of a new U.S.-Japanese equilibrium, a comprehensive revision of the alliance based on clearly defined new purposes, and a realistic process of achieving it. If incrementalism at best, or drift at worse, continues to characterize the U.S. approach to the anomalous situation in U.S.-Japanese relations, the alliance will continue to weaken in a way that is tantamount to its termination—with all the consequences of destabilizing the region and great power relations in the post–cold war world.

Some astute observers in Japan fear that an end to the alliance would have consequences similar to the termination of the Anglo-

Japanese alliance. The veteran diplomat and strategist Okazaki Hisahiko observed in 1990:

> Japan's past militarism arose from the fact that the Anglo-Japanese alliance . . . fell apart. . . . In the early years of Japan's modernization the British navy ruled the seas, providing Japan with great security. . . . But the alliance collapsed, and the Japanese had to defend themselves without outside help. When a country has to guarantee its own security, it tends to go too far for fear of falling short. And Japan did just that. Today, similarly Japan won't become militaristic as long as it has an alliance with the United States. But if Washington decides to cut the tie, I predict that in just six months we'll revert to militarism.[35]

Similarly, the veteran LDP politician Shiina Motoo, apprehensive over Japan's growing isolation following the Persian Gulf crisis, saw a parallel with the end of the Anglo-Japanese alliance. Then, as now, he wrote, Japan "set out on the path toward international isolation. Driven to pursue an overzealous defense policy, it was soon on the way toward war."[36]

American initiative in establishing a realistic new U.S.-Japanese equilibrium is necessary while Washington still maintains substantial leverage and while Japan is still divided, adrift, and reactive in its post–cold war foreign policy. This undertaking will challenge American leadership capacity because of its many dimensions. It will entail executive branch leadership and the articulation of a coherent new Japan policy based on conditions in the post–cold war world. It will require the mobilization of the considerable U.S. resources to analyze the Japanese political-economic system and devise new policies in the interest of nudging it toward a new foreign policy consensus. Above all, the path to a successful new Japan policy must inevitably lead through domestic policies that will revive American economic competitiveness.

Without American initiative an effective renewal of the alliance is not likely. Historically embedded obstacles keep Japan from taking the lead. Except in response to outside pressure, the political will, the necessary institutions, or the values and cultural resources do not exist to impel Japan to abandon its heretofore highly successful but narrowly self-generated vision of its world role. At the same time, there is a Japanese constituency for a more active international role in cooperation with the United States. This new internationalism arises less from any genuine liberalism than from a broadened conception of Japanese national interest.

As demonstrated by the gulf crisis, this view is not yet a national consensus, nor is it likely to be so for some time. Nevertheless, because it is still only partially formed, the new internationalism is tractable and susceptible to intelligent U.S. leadership.

A revised alliance will have both global and regional implications, including U.S. support and encouragement of a more prominent Japanese role in multilateral organizations, including the UN, IMF, and World Bank. In the short run, the alliance can be made more reciprocal and equal by forging a much closer cooperation on official aid projects. Joint efforts, for example, to facilitate the stability of the former eastern bloc countries and their integration into the world economy, as opposed to narrowly self-interested allocation of aid for commercial purposes, are appropriate to both countries' long-range interests.

A central purpose of the revised alliance would be cooperation in building a new structure of international relations in the Pacific and articulating its motivating spirit. Japan must play a more responsible role in regional collective security arrangements. Unless Japan is assimilated into a regional security structure, the likelihood of its adopting a more independent role, reflecting its burgeoning economic power, its robust self-confidence, and the unraveling of the U.S.-Japan alliance, will grow dramatically during the 1990s. Minimalist interpretations of Article 9, which were tolerable during the cold war, will be less persuasive both at home and abroad under the new conditions.

As for the United States, the end of the cold war, the growing economic strength of the Pacific countries, and the urgency of domestic renewal, will all generate pressure to reduce the American presence in the region. In short, the time has come to ponder the shape of a new security order in the western Pacific that is less exclusively dependent on U.S. resources. The Department of Defense has already set in motion a decrease in the size of U.S. forces, but such a decision appears driven by budgetary exigencies rather than a new strategic vision. The new conditions in Asia suggest that the U.S. approach to Asia-Pacific security should be rethought, with greater emphasis on multilateral arrangements, mutuality, consensus, and local contribution. Thought should be given to increased cooperation and coordination with Japan and other countries of the region, resulting in common military doctrine and coordinated training. In fact, some initial steps in this direction have already been taken in the 1980s, for example, greater Japanese responsibility for defense of its sea-lanes and an increased level and sophistication of joint military training with forces from the United States and other Pacific nations. In light of new conditions, moving substantially beyond these steps is appropriate. A reduced U.S. presence might lead to new forms of security maintenance, internationalized defense of sea-lanes, joint use of bases, and other new arrangements.

More than is often realized, the countries of Southeast Asia (in contrast to the countries of Northeast Asia) are evidently prepared to accept an enhanced Japanese security role, provided that the United States remains centrally involved, even at a reduced level. In April 1991, when Prime Minister Kaifu met Thai Prime Minister Anand Panyarachun, the latter said that Thailand hoped Japan would play a multifaceted role and not restrict itself solely to economic activities.[37] A year earlier the Thai prime minister had surprised Japanese officials by proposing joint Thai-Japanese naval exercises. Also in April 1991, the Philippines defense secretary proposed to members of the LDP that Asia establish a regional security system.[38] The previous month Indonesian President Suharto told Watanabe Michio, a senior LDP politician, that Indonesia would understand if Japan were to send its armed forces on overseas peace-keeping missions. Singapore's new prime minister said the same.[39] At about the same time, Malaysia tried to persuade Japan to take the lead in forming a new East Asia Economic Group, demonstrating receptivity to a more active Japanese leadership in the region.

Kaifu responded cautiously to these indications. In May 1991, on a visit to Southeast Asia, he asserted that Japan would play a greater political role in the region. This was accepted as "only natural" by Malaysian leaders and by the new prime minister of Singapore, who said that this role should be exercised within the framework of the United States security system.

With these encouraging signs of support, the Japanese made further soundings. In a lecture at the National Defense Academy, the head of the LDP's national security division, Kakizawa Koji, called for the creation of an Asian peace-keeping force:

> We have to think of discharging our responsibility to the world instead of just concentrating our efforts in developing our own economy as we did in the past; we need to apply an internationalist concept to the SDF.
>
> By bringing an "international outlook" to the SDF, I mean we should enable the SDF to build up mutual trust with other armed services in the region. This could be done through joint military exercises or through personnel exchanges with the armed forces of our neighboring

Asian countries. This is one aspect of internationalization. Another is to permit the SDF to shoulder part of the responsibility for maintaining peace and security in the Asia-Pacific region. The formation of an Asian peace-keeping force under U.N. auspices, I think, is the first step toward such internationalization.[40]

Foreign Minister Nakayama Tarō proposed at a July 1991 meeting with the ASEAN foreign ministers that an annual forum of Pacific nations be held to discuss security issues—an Asian version of the Conference on Security and Cooperation in Europe. U.S. Secretary of State James Baker showed little interest, clearly preferring the existing U.S. structure of bilateral security pacts with Japan, South Korea, Australia, Thailand, and the Philippines. Given this American reaction, the ASEAN response to Japan's proposal was ambivalent.

The United States, as the provider of security and the primary market for exports from the region, retains a good deal of leverage. While welcoming Japan's investment, aid, and technology, many Asians especially the Chinese and the Koreans, remain wary of Japan's potential domination of the region. Recognizing these concerns, Japanese policy favors a continuation of the U.S. security role as essential to maintain the stability of the region that is required for Japanese economic interests. Even in the United States, concerns growing out of the Japanese question have led many policy makers to favor an international division of labor: the United States will provide security for Asia, while Japan will provide aid. Such a solution, while necessary in the immediate future, is not viable in the long run. Japanese aid, whether or not it is formally tied to Japan's commercial interests, overwhelmingly serves them. This division of labor, even if channeled through international organizations, would leave Americans with the unpleasant and controversial role of policeman. The international, and especially U.S. reaction to Japan's simply putting up money for the gulf coalition rather than sharing in a balanced way the contributions of the international community illustrates the inadequacy of this approach.

It is not in the American interest to try to keep Japan as an abnormal country. While the Yoshida Doctrine has been largely responsible for the perpetuation of this state of affairs, the United States has been ambivalent about requesting that Japan do a great deal more in the security area out of a residual distrust of Japanese national character and memories of the militarist period. But a continuation of this "cap in the bottle" approach presumes a

145

virtual mercenary role for U.S. forces in Japan, playing the role of policeman in Asia while Japan's economic domination of the increasingly prosperous and self-assured region increases. Such an approach assures continued conflict with Japanese pride and its nationalist mood. Much of Japan exhibits an increasing impatience with a deferential foreign policy and a growing will to exert leadership in the region—in some unknown way. In the short run, if the Japanese sense that the United States would prefer Japan simply to put up more money for bases and foreign aid, then the Japanese system, given its inclination and inertia, at this point will fall into line. But such a policy of drift ignores the new realities and trends of the region and is not in accord with the long-term U.S. interest in building a structure of security suited to the new conditions.

Putting the United States at the head of the long-range trends in Asia would be more far-sighted and in the U.S. interest. Rather than attempting an indefinite containment of Japanese pride and power through a continuation of the security treaty in its present outmoded form, greater realism dictates U.S. initiative to form an organization of Pacific nations, of which a revised U.S.-Japan alliance would serve as the core. Such an organization would have many goals. It would link economic and security interests and responsibilities and be less exclusively dependent on U.S. resources than in the cold war era; it would seek the constructive engagement of China in the collective security of Asia; it would manage the downsizing of Soviet military power in the region; and it would leave the United States still retaining vast power and leverage as a balancer. Above all, with a positive Japanese security role woven into a more multilateral context, the goal of preventing an independent Japanese "power projection capability" would be achieved through positive measures rather than an effort to contain Japan through the present bilateral relationship, which is of questionable stability.

146

Notes

CHAPTER 2: THE QUESTION OF A RESURGENT JAPAN

1. Nakasone Yasuhiro, "Sōri kantei o saru ni saishite," *Bungei shunjū*, December 1987.

2. John Dower, *Empire and Aftermath: Yoshida Shigeru and the Japanese Experience, 1878–1954* (Cambridge: Harvard University Press, 1979), p. 398.

3. Theodore McNelly, "General Douglas MacArthur and the Constitutional Disarmament of Japan," in *Transactions of the Asiatic Society of Japan*, 3rd ser., vol. 17 (1982), pp. 1–34.

4. Tetsuya Kataoka, *The Price of a Constitution: The Origins of Japan's Postwar Politics* (New York: Crane Russak, 1991), p. 37.

5. Charles L. Kades, "The American Role in Revising Japan's Imperial Constitution," *Political Science Quarterly* (Summer 1989), pp. 215–47.

6. Ibid. See also Theodore H. McNelly, " 'Induced Revolution': The Policy and Process of Constitutional Reform in Occupied Japan," in Robert E. Ward and Sakamoto Yoshikazu, eds., *Democratizing Japan: The Allied Occupation* (Honolulu: University of Hawaii, 1987), pp. 76–106.

7. McNelly, " 'Induced Revolution,' " pp. 94–96.

8. Harold Brown, *Thinking about National Defense* (Boulder, Colo.: Westview Press, 1983), p. 131.

9. See *Japan Times*, July 12, 1990; also see Hiroshi Kato, "Time to Change Course," *Japan Times*, December 25, 1989.

10. See Robert C. Christopher, *The Japanese Mind* (New York: Ballantine Books, 1983), p. 55; George Ball, "We Are Playing a Dangerous Game with Japan," *New York Times Magazine*, June 25, 1972.

11. Theodore H. White, "The Danger from Japan," *New York Times Magazine*, July 29, 1985.

12. Ian Buruma, "A New Japanese Nationalism," *New York Times Magazine*, April 12, 1987.

13. Henry Scott Stokes, "Lost Samurai: The Withered Soul of Postwar Japan," *Harper's Magazine*, October 1985; Chalmers Johnson, "Reflections

on the Dilemma of Japanese Defense," *Asian Survey*, vol. 26, no. 5 (May 1986). See also Henry Scott Stokes, "Mishima, a Movie, and Nakasone," *Japan Quarterly*, vol. 31, no. 1 (January–March 1984).

14. James Fallows, "Containing Japan," *Atlantic Monthly*, May 1989.

15. R. Taggart Murphy, "Power without Purpose: The Crisis of Japan's Global Financial Dominance," *Harvard Business Review*, March–April 1989, pp. 71–83.

16. Leon Hollerman, "The Headquarters Nation," *National Interest*, Fall 1991.

17. Ishihara Shintarō and Morita Akio, *"No" to ieru Nihon* (Tokyo: Kōbunsha, 1989). See the perceptive review of this book by Shumpei Kumon in *Journal of Japanese Studies*, vol. 16, no. 2 (Summer 1990), pp. 427–36.

18. Quoted in Kei Wakaizumi, "Japan's Dilemma: To Act of Not to Act," *Foreign Policy*, vol. 16 (Fall 1974), p. 31.

19. Quoted in Tahara Soichirō, "Nippon no fumie," *Bungei shunjū*, October 1990.

20. Nakatani Iwao, " 'Nihon mondai' ga shisa suru mono," *Kokusai bunka kaikan kaihō*, October 1990.

21. *New York Times*, October 19, 1990.

22. *New York Times*, December 12, 1990.

23. Dower, *Empire and Aftermath*, pp. 277, 300.

24. See Fujio Masayuki, " 'Hōgen daijin' ōi ni hoeru," *Bungei shunjū*, October 1986.

25. See *U.S. News and World Report*, January 11, 1988, and the *Japan Times*, June 1, 1988.

26. Asai Motofumi, *Nihon gaikō hansei to tenkan* (Tokyo: Iwanami shoten, 1989), p. 158.

27. Takahashi Kamekichi, *Nihon kindai hattatsushi*, vol. 1 (Tokyo: Tōyō-keizai shimpōsha, 1973), p. 23. Professor Kozo Yamamura called my attention to this expression of Fukuzawa's views.

28. Dower, *Empire and Aftermath*, p. 289.

29. Ibid., p. 290.

CHAPTER 3: JAPAN'S POSTWAR NATIONAL PURPOSE

1. See the excellent biography of Yoshida by John W. Dower, *Empire and Aftermath: Yoshida Shigeru and the Japanese Experience, 1878–1954* (Cambridge: Harvard University Press, 1979).

2. Kōsaka Masataka, *Saishō Yoshida Shigeru* (Tokyo: Chūō kōronsha, 1968), p. 5.

3. Dower, *Empire and Aftermath*, pp. 380–81. Italics added.

4. See U.S. Department of State, *Foreign Relations of the United States, 1950*, vol. 6 (Washington, D.C.: DoS, 1966), pp. 1166–67.

5. Henry Kissinger, *White House Years* (Boston: Little, Brown, 1979), p. 324.

6. Michael M. Yoshitsu, *Japan and the San Francisco Peace Settlement* (New York: Columbia University Press, 1983), pp. 53–54.

7. See T. J. Pempel, ed., *Uncommon Democracies: The One-Party Dominant Regimes* (Ithaca, N.Y.: Cornell University Press, 1990), p. 139.

8. Yōnosuke Nagai, "U.S.–Japan Relations in the Global Context," (Unpublished paper, 1983).

9. William J. Sebald, *With MacArthur in Japan: A Personal History of the Occupation* (New York: W. W. Norton, 1965), pp. 257–58; Dower, *Empire and Aftermath*, p. 383.

10. Igarashi Takeshi, "Sengo Nihon 'gaikō jōsei' no keisei," *Kokka gakkai zasshi*, no. 5–8 (1984), p. 486.

11. Chihiro Hosoya, "Japan's Response to U.S. Policy on the Japanese Peace Treaty," *Hitotsubashi Journal of Law and Politics*, vol. 10 (1981), p. 18.

12. Dower, *Empire and Aftermath*, p. 315.

13. Ibid., pp. 364, 372.

14. Miyazawa Kiichi, *Tokyo-Washington no mitsudan* (Tokyo: Jitsugyō no Nihonsha, 1956), p. 160. Also see Tetsuya Kataoka, *The Price of a Constitution: The Origin of Japan's Postwar Politics* (New York: Crane Russak, 1991), p. 118.

15. Yoshitsu, *Japan and the Peace Settlement*, p. 40.

16. Yoshida Shigeru, *Sekai to Nippon* (Tokyo: Banchō shobō, 1963), pp. 202–203.

17. Translated in *Journal of Social and Political Ideas in Japan*, vol. 3, no. 2 (1965), pp. 49–65.

18. Masataka Kōsaka, "The Quest for Credibility," *Look Japan*, September 10, 1981.

19. John Welfield, *An Empire in Eclipse* (London: Athlone Press, 1988), pp. 97–98.

20. Ibid., p. 99.

21. Ibid., p. 107.

22. Nagai Yōnosuke, *Gendai to senryaku* (Tokyo: Bungei shunjū, 1985), p. 60. See also Welfield, *Empire in Eclipse*, p. 104.

23. Quoted in Kataoka, *Price of a Constitution*, pp. 122–23.

24. Pempel, *Uncommon Democracies*, p. 142.

25. Takafusa Nakamura, *The Postwar Japanese Economy: Its Development and Structure* (Tokyo: University of Tokyo Press, 1981), pp. 80–81.

26. Akira Iriye and Warren I. Cohen, eds., *The United States and Japan in the Postwar World* (Lexington: University of Kentucky Press, 1989), p. 97.

27. Welfield, *Empire in Eclipse*, p. 242.

28. Ibid., p. 251.

29. Ibid., p. 210. See also Chalmers Johnson's review of Welfield in the *Journal of Japanese Studies*, vol. 16, no. 1, pp. 258–62.

30. Richard Solomon and Masataka Kōsaka, *The Soviet Far East Military Buildup* (Dover, Mass.: Auburn House, 1986), p. 136.

31. " 'Nori-okure' gaikō no susume," *Chūō kōron*, March 1980.

32. Tahara Soichirō, "Sōren wa kowai desu ka," *Bungei shunjū*, March 1980.

33. Amaya Naohiro, *Nippon wa doko e iku no ka* (Tokyo: PHP, 1989), p. 189.

34. Nishio Kanji, "Senryaku toshite no 'sakoku' e no ishi," *Seiron*, January 1988.

35. Kōsaka Masataka, *Bunmei ga suibō suru toki* (Tokyo: Shinchosha, 1981), p. 268.

36. Kōsaka Masataka, "Tsūshō kokka Nihon no unmei," *Chūō kōron*, November 1975.

37. Amaya Naohiro, "Chōnin koku Nihon tedai no kurigoto," *Bungei shunjū*, March 1980; for a partial translation of this essay, see *Japan Echo*, vol. 7, no. 2 (1980), pp. 53–62. See also idem, "Nichi-Bei jidōsha mondai to chōnin kokka," *Bungei shunjū*, June 1980, and "Sōpu nashonarizumu o haisu," *Bungei shunjū*, July 1981.

38. Nagai Yōnosuke, "Moratoriamu kokka no bōei ron," *Chūō kōron*, January 1981.

39. Igarashi Takeshi, "Peace-Making and Party Politics: The Formation of the Domestic Foreign-Policy System in Postwar Japan," *Journal of Japanese Studies*, vol. 2, no. 2 (Summer 1985), pp. 323–56.

40. Nagai, *Gendai to senryaku*, p. 67.

Chapter 4: Competing Views of Japanese Purpose

1. Akira Iriye, *Power and Culture: The Japanese-American War* (Cambridge: Harvard University Press, 1981), p. 259.

2. Sakakibara Eisuke and Noguchi Yukio, "Ōkurashō—Nichigin ōchō no bunseki," *Chūō kōron*, August 1977, p. 113.

3. Matsumoto Sannosuke, "The Significance of Nationalism in Modern Japanese Thought: Some Theoretical Problems," *Journal of Asian Studies*, vol. 31, no. 1 (November 1971), pp. 49–56.

4. Michael A. Barnhart, *Japan Prepares for Total War: The Search for Economic Security 1919–1941* (Ithaca, N.Y.: Cornell University Press, 1987), p. 273.

5. Sakakibara and Noguchi, "Ōkurashō." Translation from *Japan Echo*, vol. 4, no. 4 (1977), pp. 88–124.

6. See Daniel I. Okimoto and Thomas P. Rohlen, eds., *Inside the Japanese System* (Stanford, Calif.: Stanford University Press, 1988), p. 80.

7. Kōsaka Masataka, "Tsūshō kokka Nihon no unmei," *Chūō kōron*, November 1975.

8. See Michio Muramatsu and Ellis S. Krauss, "The Conservative Policy Line and the Development of Patterned Pluralism," in Kozo Yamamura and Yasukichi Yasuba, eds., *The Political Economy of Japan*, vol. 1, *The Domestic Transformation* (Stanford, Calif.: Stanford University Press, 1987), pp. 516–54.

9. Komiya Ryūtarō, "Ureubeki migi senkai," *Gendai keizai*, vol. 6 (Spring 1979), pp. 71–84.

10. Ijiri Kazuo, "Chishikijin to 99-hiki no mayoeru hitsujitachi," *Voice*, July 1979; see translation in *Japan Echo*, vol. 6, no. 3 (1979), pp. 85–92.

11. Maruyama Masao, *Thought and Behavior in Modern Japanese Politics* (Oxford: Oxford University Press, 1969), p. 307.

12. Kamishima Jirō, "Hibusō-shugi—sono dentō to genjitsusei," *Sekai*, July 1980.

13. Tsuru Shigeto, "Whither Japan? A Positive Program of Nation-Building in an Age of Uncertainty," *Japan Quarterly*, vol. 27, no. 4 (1980), pp. 487–98.

14. Sakamoto Yoshikazu, "Japan's Role in World Politics," *Japan Quarterly*, vol. 27, no. 2 (1980), pp. 166–73.

15. Iida Tsuneo, *Nippon-teki chikara-zuyosa no sai-hakken* (Nihon keizai shinbunsha, 1979), p. 206.

16. See Tetsuo Anzai, "We Can Still Learn from Europe," *Japan Echo*, vol. 2, no. 1 (1975), pp. 128–29.

17. Kimura Harumi, "Nihon wa Eikoku-byō ni kakarenai," *Shokun*, April 1977; see translation in *Japan Echo*, vol. 4, no. 2 (1977), p. 51.

18. Shimomura Mitsuko, " 'Eikō aru Amerika' wa doko ni," *Voice*, September 1980; see translation in *Japan Echo*, vol. 8, no. 1 (1991), pp. 119–22.

19. Kondo Ken, "Amerika wa itsu yomigaeru ka," *Voice*, December 1980; see translation in *Japan Echo*, vol. 8, no. 1 (1981), pp. 65–66.

20. Okazaki Hisahiko, "Amerika wa tayori ni naru ka," *Voice*, July 1979; see translation in *Japan Echo*, vol. 6, no. 3 (1979), pp. 32–40.

21. "Bunka jidai no keizai unei kenkyū gurūpu," *Hōkoku-sho*, July 12, 1980, p. 72.

22. Ibid., p. 81.

23. Ibid., p. 87.

24. Amaya Naohiro, "Dokkin-hō kaisei shian ni hanron suru," *Ekonomisuto*, November 19, 1974.

25. Iida Tsuneo, *Nippon-teki chikara-zuyosa*, p. 79.

26. Amaya, "Dokkin-hō kaisei."

27. Ibid.

28. Amaya Naohiro, "Wa no rinri to dokkin hō no ronri," *Bungei shunjū*, December 1980.

29. Iida, *Nippon-teki chikara-zuyosa*, p. 2.

30. Ibid., p. 31.

31. Ibid., p. 31.

32. Quoted in Ōtake Hideo, *Saigunbi to nashonarizumu* (Tokyo: Chūō kōronsha, 1988), p. 133.

33. Ibid., p. 134.

34. Ibid., pp. 136–37.

35. See the discussion between Shiina's son, Shiina Motoo, and Okazaki Hisahiko in "Dare no tame ni bōei-hi 'GNP 1%' rongi ka," *Shokun*, January 1985.

36. Etō Jun, *1946-nen kempō: sono kōsoku* (Tokyo: Bungeishunjūsha, 1980), p. 92.

37. Etō Jun, " 'Yoshida-seiji' o minaosu," *Seiron*, September 1983.

38. Etō, *1946 kempō*, p. 100.

39. Katsuda Kichitarō, *Heiwa kempō o utagau* (Tokyo: Kōdansha, 1981), p. 149.

40. Ibid., p. 143.

41. Shimizu Ikutarō, *Nippon yo, kokka tare: Kaku no sentaku* (Tokyo: Bungeishunjūsha, 1980), pp. 65–66.

42. Ibid., p. 86.

43. Ibid., p. 91.

44. Ibid., p. 83.

45. Ibid., p. 89.

46. Etō Jun, *Nichi-Bei sensō wa owatte inai* (Tokyo: Bungeishunjū, 1987), pp. 204–6.

47. *"No" to ieru Nippon* (Tokyo: Kōbunsha, 1989); the translated passages here are from Ishihara, "No wa no de aru," *Bungei shunjū*, November 1989. See translation in *Japan Echo*, vol. 17, no. 1 (Spring 1990).

48. Yasusuke Murakami, " 'New Middle Mass' Japanese: Where Do We Go from Here?" *Look Japan*, January 10, 1985.

CHAPTER 5: A NEW DEFINITION OF NATIONAL INTEREST

1. Ōtake Hideo, "Nakasone seiji no ideorogi," *Leviathan* (Autumn 1987), p. 83.

2. *Nikkei bijinesu*, February 22, 1982, p. 193.

3. See James C. Abegglen, "Narrow Self-Interest: Japan's Ultimate Vulnerability," in Diane Tasca, ed., *U.S.-Japanese Economic Relations: Cooperation, Competition, and Confrontation* (Pergamon Press, 1980), p. 27.

4. Suzuki Sunao, "Intellectual Climate and Policy-Making," *Japan Quarterly*, vol. 27, no. 2 (1980), pp. 174–79.

5. Itō Kenichi, " 'Mai hōmu gaikō' no jidai wa owatta," *Asahi janaru*, February 15, 1980. See also Itō Kenichi, *Amerika wa yomigaeru ka?* (Tokyo: Gōdō Shuppan, 1980), pp. 319–36.

6. See Edward Seidensticker, *This Country, Japan* (Tokyo: Kodansha, 1984), pp. 331–32.

7. Edwin O. Reischauer, *The Japanese* (Cambridge: Harvard University Press, 1978), p. 420.

8. Dan F. Henderson, "Access to the Japanese Market: Some Aspects of Foreign Exchange Controls and Banking Law," in Gary R. Saxonhouse and Kozo Yamamura, eds., *Law and Trade Issues of the Japanese Economy* (Seattle: University of Washington Press, 1986), p. 133.

9. See Reischauer's introduction to Seizaburo Sato, Ken'ichi Koyama, and Shunpei Kumon, eds., *Postwar Politician: The Life of Former Prime Minister Masayoshi Ohira* (Tokyo: Kodansha, 1990).

10. Quoted in Nagatomi Yūichirō, *Kindai o koeru* (Tokyo: Ōkurazaimu kyōkai, 1983), vol. 2, p. 445.

11. See Nagatomi, *Kindai o koeru*, vol. 1, p. 2. See also *Ōhira Masayoshi kaisōroku* (Tokyo: Kagoshima shuppankai, 1983), pp. 483–94.

12. *Japan Times*, January 26, 1980.

13. Nagatomi, *Kindai o koeru*, vol. 1, pp. 6–8.

14. Ibid., vol. 1, pp. 31–33.

15. Yuichiro Nagatomi, ed., *Masayoshi Ohira's Proposal to Evolve the Global Society* (Tokyo: Foundation for Advanced Information and Research, 1988), p. 718.

16. These research teams published their reports in a series entitled *Sofutonomikksu fuoroappu kenkyūkai hōkokusho* (Tokyo: Ōkurashō, 1985–1989).

17. Ōtake, "Nakasone seiji no ideorogi," pp. 73–91.

18. Sakakibara Eisuke and Noguchi Yukio, "Ōkurashō—Nichigin ōchō no bunseki," *Chūō kōron*, August 1977, p. 113.

19. "Takumashii bunka to fukushi no kuni o," *Seiron*, January 1983. Translation in *Japan Echo*, vol. 10, no. 1, Spring 1983. In *Nihon keizai shimbun*, July 8, 1983, Nakasone attributed these ideas to Ōhira's Research Groups. See Aoki Satoshi, *Rinkyōshin kaitai* (Tokyo: Akebi shobō, 1986), p. 102.

20. Nagatomi, *Masayoshi Ohira's Proposal*, p. 538.

21. Ōhira sōri no seisaku kenkyūkai, ed., *Bunka no jidai* (Tokyo: Ōkurashō, 1988), p. 71.

22. Ōhira sōri no seisaku kenkyū, ed., *Sōgō anzen hōsho senryaku* (Tokyo: Ōkurashō, 1980), pp. 7–10.

23. Chalmers Johnson, *MITI and the Japanese Miracle* (Stanford, Calif.: Stanford University Press, 1982), p. 263.

24. Ryutaro Komiya and Motoshige Itoh, "Japan's International Trade and Trade Policy, 1955–1984," in Takashi Inoguchi and Daniel I. Okimoto, eds., *The Political Economy of Japan*, vol. 2: *The Changing International Context* (Stanford, Calif.: Stanford University Press, 1988) pp. 182–85.

25. Johnson, *MITI and the Japanese Miracle*, p. 281.

26. Ibid., p. 302; Henderson, "Access to the Japanese Market," pp. 131–46.

27. Komiya and Itoh, "Japan's International Trade," p. 185.

28. Ibid., pp. 213–14.

29. Nagatomi, *Ohira's Proposal*, pp. 51–52, 59, 89.

30. Keizai kikakushō, ed., *2000-nen no Nihon: kokusaika, koreika, seijukuka ni sonaete* (Tokyo: 1982), introduction.

31. See *Sekai no naka no Nihon o kangaeru* (Tokyo: Tsūshō sangyō chōsakai, 1986). The report has been translated: Murakami Yasusuke and Kosai Yutaka, eds., *Japan in the Global Community: Its Role and Contribution on the Eve of the Twenty-first Century* (Tokyo: University of Tokyo Press, 1986), p. 69.

32. Ibid., pp. 69–71.

33. Ibid., p. 9.

34. Ibid., p. 35.

35. *Sōgō anzen hoshō senryaku*; see also Nagatomi, *Ohira's Proposal*, pp. 224, 237.

36. Murakami and Kosai, eds., *Japan in the Global Community*, pp. 36–37.

37. Ibid., p. 34.

38. Gary R. Saxonhouse, "Comparative Advantage, Structural Adaptation, and Japanese Performance," in Inoguchi and Okimoto, *The Political Economy of Japan*, vol. 2, p. 246.

39. Robert Gilpin, *The Political Economy of International Relations* (Princeton: Princeton University Press, 1987), pp. 391–92.

40. Saxonhouse, "Comparative Advantage," pp. 246–47.

41. Ōtake, "Nakasone seiji no ideorogi," *Leviathan* (Autumn 1987), p. 83.

42. Murakami and Kosai, eds., *Japan in the Global Community*, p. 118.

43. Ernest R. May, *Imperial Democracy: The Emergence of America as a Great Power* (New York: Harcourt Brace, 1961), p. 270.

44. Marius B. Jansen, "Modernization and Foreign Policy in Meiji Japan," in Robert E. Ward, ed., *Political Development in Modern Japan* (Princeton: Princeton University Press, 1968), p. 159.

CHAPTER 6: THE STRUGGLE TO REORIENT JAPANESE PURPOSE

1. See Teruhisa Horio, *Educational Thought and Ideology in Modern Japan* (Tokyo: University of Tokyo Press, 1988), pp. 375, 365, and 378.

2. See Watanabe Osamu, "The Emperor as a 'Symbol' in Postwar Japan," *Acta Asiatica*, no. 59 (1990), pp. 101–25.

3. Nakasone Yasuhiro, *My Life in Politics* (1982) (typescript). A copy of Nakasone's petition to General MacArthur is in the Justin Williams Papers, University of Maryland Library.

4. Sase Masamori, "Nihon gaikō no tokushu-sei o tsuku," *Voice*, July 1981.

5. Kōyama Ken'ichi, "Nippon-kei 'seijuku shakai' no shinario," *Voice*, February 1983.

6. Yamamoto Tsuyoshi, "Hoshu seiji no tokushitsu to Nakasone gaikō," *Sekai*, July 16, 1986.

7. George R. Packard, "The Dimensions of Nakasone's Triumph," *New York Times*, July 16, 1986.

8. Nakasone Yasuhiro, "Takumashii bunka to fukushi no kuni o," *Seiron*, January 1983, pp. 26–37. See translation in *Japan Echo*, vol. 10, no. 1 (1983), pp. 12–18.

9. *Japan Times*, January 10, 1984.

10. Analysis of the Maekawa Report is found in Kenneth B. Pyle, ed., *The Trade Crisis: How Will Japan Respond?* (Seattle: Society for Japanese Studies, 1987).

11. Ibid., p. 39.

12. Murakami Yasusuke and Kosai Yutaka, eds., *Japan in the Global Community: Its Role and Contribution on the Eve of the Twenty-first Century* (Tokyo: University of Tokyo Press, 1986), p. 34.

13. The full text of Nakasone's remarks was published in *Chūō kōron*, November 1986. I have used William Wetherall's excellent analysis and partial translation of this text from the *Japan Times*, November 26, 1986.

14. U. Alexis Johnson, *The Right Hand of Power* (Englewood Cliffs, N.J.: Prentice-Hall, 1984), p. 521; Marvin Kalb and Bernard Kalb, *Kissinger* (Boston: Little, Brown, 1974), p. 255; Albrecht Rothacher, *Economic Diplomacy between the European Community and Japan, 1959–1981* (Aldershot, Eng.: Gower, 1989), p. 257.

15. Hasegawa Michiko, "Sengo sedai ni totte no dai-Tōa sensō," *Chūō kōron*, April 1983. See translation in *Japan Echo*, vol. 11, special issue (1984), pp. 29–37.

16. Yoshida Mitsuru, "Shisha no migawari no sedai," *Shokun*, November 1979. See translation in *Japan Echo*, vol. 7, no. 2 (1980), p. 79.

17. See the careful study of Leonard James Schoppa, *Education Reform in Japan: A Case of Immobilist Politics* (London: Routledge, 1991), pp. 215–23.

18. *Japan Times*, April 24, 1986.

19. "Mirai shikō ka, genjitsu-shugi ka," *Chūō kōron*, April 1985. See translation in *Japan Echo*, vol. 12, no. 2 (1985), p. 52.

20. Kōyama, "Kakuitsu sei ni shi o," *Next*, March 1985. Translation in *Japan Echo*, vol. 12, no. 2 (1985), p. 45.

21. *Japan Times*, April 24, 1986.

22. Murakami and Kosai, eds., *Japan in the Global Community*, pp. 27–29.

23. See "Nakasone seiji wa nani o shita no ka!" *Asahi janaru*, June 20, 1986. The Yasukuni issue is one of a range of issues important to the "New Right." See Hori Yukio, *Sengo no uyoku seiryoku* (Tokyo: Keiso shobō, 1983).

24. See Wetherall's translation, *Japan Times*, November 26, 1986.

25. *Japan Economic Journal*, October 11, 1986.

26. *Washington Post*, January 19, 1983; see also Don Oberdorfer, "How Nakasone Lost Control of His 'Carrier,' " reprinted in *Japan Times*, March 23, 1983.

27. *Mainichi shimbun*, July 17, 1986. Translation by Asia Foundation Translation Service Center.

28. Kōsaka Masataka, "Yaruta taisei: yonjū-nen: Nihon gaikō no kijiku wa dō kawaru ka," *Chūō kōron*, January 1985. For a more elaborate explanation of Kōsaka's advocacy of a merchant role for Japan in the world, see his book *Bunmei ga suibō suru toki* (Tokyo: Shinchō-sha, 1981), pp. 243–70.

CHAPTER 7: THE BURDENS OF HISTORY

1. In an article on Nakasone's "grand design" for reorienting Japan's international role, I described the prime minister as caught between the

past and the future in trying to lead his country toward a more activist foreign policy. In a speech to the Asia Foundation in San Francisco, March 10, 1988, Nakasone agreed with this assessment and expressed impatience with the pace of change:

> Professor Pyle argues that [I] expounded a grand design for transforming Japan's foreign policy—namely, from a policy of traditional passivity to one in which Japan carries growing international responsibilities, involves itself in strategic issues, plays an active role in its national defense, and is supported by a new and liberal nationalism. Although I agree with the way Professor Pyle has formulated the basic design of my foreign policy, the outcome of that design is yet to be seen.

Kenneth B. Pyle, "The Burden of Japanese History and the Politics of Burden Sharing," in John H. Makin and Donald C. Hellmann, eds., *Sharing World Leadership? A New Era for America and Japan* (Washington, D.C.: American Enterprise Institute, 1989), p. 46.

2. Robert Gilpin, *The Political Economy of International Relations* (Princeton: Princeton University Press, 1987), pp. 389–90.

3. Leonard James Schoppa, *Education Reform in Japan: A Case of Immobilist Policies* (London: Routledge, 1991), pp. 234–247.

4. Michael Mandelbaum, *The Fate of Nations: The Search for National Security in the Nineteenth and Twentieth Centuries* (Cambridge: Cambridge University Press, 1988), p. 380.

5. Inoguchi Takashi, "Zokueki, shōeki ga naiju kakudai o sogai suru," *Ekonomisuto*, September 8, 1987; see translation in *Japan Echo*, vol. 14, no. 4 (1987), pp. 56–58. See also Inoguchi and Iwai Tomoaki, *'Zokugiin' no kenkyū* (Tokyo: Nihon keizaishimbunsha, 1987).

6. Nakatani Iwao, "Sekinin kokka, Nihon e no sentaku," *Asuteion*, Autumn 1987; see translation in *Japan Echo*, vol. 14, no. 4 (1987), pp. 7–18.

7. Gotō Noboru, "Watakushi no Nihon keizai kaizo an," *Bungei shunjū*, July 1988.

8. Sakakibara Eisuke, "Is Japan Governable?" *International Economy*, May/June 1988, pp. 92–99.

9. Ryutaro Komiya and Motoshige Itoh, "Japan's International Trade and Trade Policy, 1955–1984," in Takashi Inoguchi and Daniel I. Okimoto, eds., *The Political Economy of Japan*, vol. 2, *The Changing International Context* (Stanford, Calif.: Stanford University Press, 1988), p. 210.

10. Daniel I. Okimoto, "Political Inclusivity: The Domestic Structure of Trade," in Inoguchi and Okimoto, *Political Economy of Japan*, vol. 2, pp. 334–37.

11. Komiya and Itoh, p. 210.

12. Murakami Yasusuke, "The Japanese Model of Political Economy," in Kozo Yamamura and Yasukichi Yasuba, eds., *The Political Economy of Japan*, vol. 1, *The Domestic Transformation* (Stanford, Calif.: Stanford University Press, 1987), pp. 89–90.

13. *Look Japan*, September 10, 1986, p. 4.

14. Otsuka Kazuhiko, "Charting a New Policy Course," *Economic Eye*, June 1986.

15. Inoguchi, "Zokueki."

16. Tanaka Naoki, "The Nakasone Legacy," *Economic Eye*, December 1987.

17. George C. Eads and Kozo Yamamura, "The Future of Industrial Policy," in Yamamura and Yasukichi Yasuba, eds., *The Political Economy of Japan*, vol. 1, *The Domestic Transformation* (Stanford: Stanford University Press, 1987), p. 466.

18. *Japan Economic Journal*, January 31, 1987.

19. See Schoppa, *Education Reform in Japan*, p. 254.

20. *Sekai no naka no Nihon o kangaeru* (Tokyo: Tsūshō sangyō chōsakai, 1986). See translation: Yasusuke Murakami and Yutaka Kosai, eds., *Japan in the Global Community* (Tokyo: University of Tokyo Press, 1986), pp. 113–14.

21. Hasegawa Michiko, " 'Kokusaika' to iu kotoba o saiko suru," *Shokun*, December 1985; translation in *Japan Echo*, vol. 13, no. 3 (1986), pp. 49–55.

22. Nishio Kanji, "Senryaku toshite no 'sakoku' e no ishi," *Seiron*, January 1988.

23. Shimomura Osamu, *Nippon wa waruku nai: warui no wa Amerika da* (Tokyo: Bungei shunju, 1987).

24. Takeuchi Hirotaka, "Jinteki sakoku taisei kara dappi seyo," *Chūō kōron*, October 1987.

25. Yamazaki Masakazu, "Nihon bunka no rekishiteki jikken," *Chūō kōron*, June 1986; translation in *Japan Echo*, vol. 13, no. 3 (1986), pp. 56–63.

26. Satō Seizaburō, "Kokusaika e no Nihon no kakugo," *Seiron*, November 1987.

27. Amaya Naohiro, "The Dawning of a New Era," *Speaking of Japan*, vol. 9, no. 89 (May 1988), pp. 21–22.

28. Yano Tōru, *Kokusaika no imi* (Tokyo: NHK Bukkusu, 1986); see also the essays by Yano in *Japan Times*, September 28 and 29, 1986.

29. Charles Kindleberger, *The World in Depression, 1929–1939* (Berkeley: University of California Press, 1973), chaps. 1 and 14.

30. Robert Gilpin, *U.S. Power and the Multinational Corporation: The Political Economy of Direct Foreign Investment* (New York: Basic Books, 1975), p. 84.

31. John Gallagher and Ronald Robinson, "The Imperialism of Free Trade," *Economic History Review*, vol. 6, no. 1 (1953), pp. 1–15.

32. Gilpin, *Political Economy of International Relations*, pp. 182–85.

33. Japan, of course, did not have tariff autonomy at this time. Marlene Mayo, "Rationality in the Meiji Restoration," in Bernard Silberman and H. D. Harootunian, eds., *Modern Japanese Leadership* (Tucson: University of Arizona Press, 1966), p. 344.

34. Quoted in Clyde V. Prestowitz, Jr., *Trading Places: How We Allowed Japan to Take the Lead* (New York: Basic Books, 1988), p. 272.

35. David P. Calleo and Benjamin M. Rowland, *America and the World Political Economy* (Bloomington: Indiana University Press, 1973), p. 58.

36. Amaya Naohiro, "Japan azu nanba tsū," *Voice*, May 1984. Also see Amaya, *Nippon wa doko e iku no ka* (Tokyo: PHP, 1989), pp. 201–5.

37. Kōsaka Masataka, "Nichibei 'tokubetsu kankei' no honshitsu," *Voice*, January 1988.

38. Murakami, "Japanese Model of Political Economy," in Yamamura and Yasuba, eds., *The Political Economy of Japan*, p. 85.

39. Tsūshōsangyōshō Daijin Kanbō, ed., *Nihon no sentaku* (Tokyo: MITI, 1988), pp. 30–35. See also Shinji Fukukawa, "Japan's Choices," *Look Japan* (November 1988).

40. Amaya Naohiro, "Saraba, chōnin kokka," *Voice*, October 1987; three years later he published a collection of essays under the same title: Amaya Naohiro, *Saraba, chōnin kokka* (Tokyo: PHP, 1990).

41. *Tōkyō shimbun*, June 24, 1987. Asia Foundation Translation Service.

42. See Shimada Haruo, "Imakoso kigyō kōdō ni aratana kachi kijin o," *Chūō kōron*, May 1990; translated as "The Desperate Need for New Values," *Journal of Japanese Studies*, vol. 17, no. 1 (Winter 1991). See also Kozo Yamamura, "Will Japan's Economic Structure Change?" in Yamamura, ed., *Japan's Economic Structure: Should It Change?* (Seattle: Society for Japanese Studies, 1990), pp. 13–64.

CHAPTER 8: POWER AND PURPOSE IN A NEW ERA

1. Amaya Naohiro, *Nippon wa doko e iku no ka* (Tokyo: PHP, 1989), p. 189.

2. See Murakami's editorial introduction to *Japan Echo*, vol. 17, no. 4 (1990), p. 4.

3. Michael M. Yoshitsu, *Japan and the San Francisco Peace Settlement* (New York: Columbia University Press, 1983), pp. 53–54.

4. Miyazawa Kiichi, *Tokyo-Washington no mitsudan* (Tokyo: Jitsugyō no Nihonsha, 1956), p. 160.

5. John Welfield, *An Empire in Eclipse* (London: Athlone Press, 1988), p. 251.

6. Nishio Kanji, "Senryaku toshite no 'sakoku' e no ishi," *Seiron*, January 1988.

7. Richard Solomon and Masataka Kosaka, *The Soviet Far East Military Buildup* (Dover, Mass.: Auburn House, 1986), p. 137.

8. *New York Times*, April 5, 1991.

9. Charles Kades, "The American Role in Revising Japan's Imperial Constitution," *Political Science Quarterly*, Summer 1989, p. 237.

10. Tahara Soichirō, "Nippon no fumie," *Bungei shunjū*, October 1990.

11. *Yomiuri*, October 13, 1990. See translation in Itō Kenichi, "The

Japanese State of Mind: Deliberations on the Gulf Crisis," *Journal of Japanese Studies*, vol. 17, no. 2 (Summer 1991), p. 282.

12. Nakasone Yasuhiro and Kōsaka Masataka, "Atarashii Nippon no kokka senryaku," *Voice*, May 1991.

13. Tahara Soichirō, "Sōren wa kowai desu ka," *Bungei shunjū* (March 1980); Miyazawa Kiichi and Kōsaka Masataka, *Utsukushii Nihon e no chōsen* (Tokyo: Bungei shunjū, 1984); Tahara Soichirō, "Nippon no fumie," *Bungei shunjū* (October 1990).

14. Asian Development Bank, *Asian Development Outlook* (Manila: ADB, 1990), pp. 39–41.

15. *Japan Times*, June 8, 1991.

16. See David Arase, "U.S. and ASEAN Perceptions of Japan's Role in the Asian-Pacific Region," and Steven C. M. Wong, "Japan in Search of a Global Economic Role," in Harry H. Kendall and Clara Joewono, eds., *Japan, ASEAN, and the United States* (Berkeley, Calif.: Institute of East Asian Studies, 1991), pp. 275, 296–97.

17. Ibid., p. 273.

18. *Asian Wall Street Journal*, August 21, 1990.

19. Foundation for Advanced Information and Research, *Interim Report of Asia-Pacific Economic Research* (Tokyo: FAIR, 1990), pp. 217, 226.

20. Ibid., pp. 232–33.

21. Susumu Awanohara, "Japan and East Asia: Toward a New Division of Labor," *Pacific Review*, vol. 2, no. 3 (1989).

22. Foundation for Advanced Information and Research, *Interim Report*, p. 164.

23. *New York Times*, August 5, 1991.

24. Arase, "U.S. and ASEAN Perceptions of Japan's Role," p. 269.

25. See Robert M. Orr, Jr., *The Emergence of Japan's Foreign Aid Power* (New York: Columbia University Press, 1990).

26. See *Economist*, July 15, 1989; see also Arase, "U.S. and ASEAN Perceptions of Japan's Role."

27. *Asian Wall Street Journal*, June 4, 1991.

28. Inoguchi Takashi, "Japan's Response to the Gulf Crisis: An Analytic Overview," *Journal of Japanese Studies*, vol. 17, no. 2 (Summer 1991), p. 261.

29. Interview with Ishihara in *Time*, November 20, 1989, p. 82.

30. Yasusuke Murakami, "The Debt Comes Due for Mass Higher Education," *Japan Echo*, vol. 15, no. 3 (Autumn 1988), pp. 71–80.

31. For a similar but broader vision of structural change in international politics, see Zbigniew Brzezinski, "Selective Global Commitment," *Foreign Affairs*, vol. 70, no. 4 (Fall 1991), pp. 1–20.

32. John W. Dower, *Empire and Aftermath: Yoshida Shigeru and the Japanese Experience, 1878–1954* (Cambridge: Harvard University Press, 1979), p. 36.

33. See the testimony of Donald C. Hellmann before the U.S. Congress, Senate, Foreign Relations Committee, 102nd Congress, 1st session, October 31, 1991.

34. Dower, *Empire and Aftermath*, p. 307.

35. Okazaki Hisahiko and Satō Seizaburō, "Nihon wa kokusaiteki sekinin o dō hatatsu no ka," in *Gaikō Forum*, October 1990. See translation in *Japan Echo*, vol. 18, no. 1 (Spring 1991).

36. Shiina Motoo, "Kokuren gaikō ka Nichi-Bei dōmei ka," in *Chūō kōron*, November 1990. See translation in *Japan Echo*, vol. 18, no. 1 (Spring 1991).

37. See Okazaki Hisahiko, "Ajia shokoku e no hairyo," *Voice*, July 1991.

38. *Japan Times*, April 4, 1991.

39. *Economist*, March 9, 1991.

40. *Japan Times*, April 17, 1991.

Index

About the Author

Kenneth B. Pyle is professor of history and Asian studies at the University of Washington. From 1978 to 1988 he was also director of the Henry M. Jackson School of International Studies there. He is the author or editor of several books on modern Japan and its international relations, including *The New Generation in Meiji Japan* (1969), *The Making of Modern Japan* (1978), and *The Trade Crisis: How Will Japan Respond?* (1987).

Mr. Pyle was editor of the *Journal of Japanese Studies* from its founding in 1974 to 1986. He is president of the recently established National Bureau of Asian Research and a member of the Board of Governors of the Henry M. Jackson Foundation (since 1983). Mr. Pyle is vice chairman of the Japan–U.S. Friendship Commission, a federal agency that administers a trust fund, established by Congress at the time of the reversion of Okinawa, to support Japanese studies. He was a board member of the Maureen and Mike Mansfield Foundation (1981–1988).

The author took his B.A. *magna cum laude* from Harvard College (1958) and his Ph.D. from Johns Hopkins University (1965), where he was the Walter Hines Page Fellow in International Relations. He held a Ford Foundation fellowship at the Interuniversity Center for Japanese Studies in Tokyo (1961–1964). Mr. Pyle has been a visiting faculty member at Stanford and Yale Universities.

Samuel P. Huntington
Eaton Professor of the
Science of Government
Harvard University

D. Gale Johnson
Eliakim Hastings Moore
Distinguished Service Professor
of Economics Emeritus
University of Chicago

William M. Landes
Clifton R. Musser Professor of
Economics
University of Chicago Law School

Sam Peltzman
Sears Roebuck Professor of Economics
and Financial Services
University of Chicago
Graduate School of Business

Nelson W. Polsby
Professor of Political Science
University of California at Berkeley

Murray L. Weidenbaum
Mallinckrodt Distinguished
University Professor
Washington University

Research Staff

Claude E. Barfield
Resident Scholar

Walter Berns
Adjunct Scholar

Douglas J. Besharov
Resident Scholar

Robert H. Bork
John M. Olin Scholar in Legal Studies

Anthony R. Dolan
Visiting Fellow

Dinesh D'Souza
Research Fellow

Nicholas N. Eberstadt
Visiting Scholar

Mark Falcoff
Resident Scholar

Gerald R. Ford
Distinguished Fellow

Murray F. Foss
Visiting Scholar

Suzanne Garment
Resident Scholar

Patrick Glynn
Resident Scholar

Robert A. Goldwin
Resident Scholar

Gottfried Haberler
Resident Scholar

Robert W. Hahn
Resident Scholar

Robert B. Helms
Visiting Scholar

Leon Kass
W. H. Brady
Distinguished Fellow

Karlyn H. Keene
Resident Fellow; Editor,
The American Enterprise

Jeane J. Kirkpatrick
Senior Fellow

Marvin H. Kosters
Resident Scholar; Director,
Economic Policy Studies

Irving Kristol
John M. Olin Distinguished Fellow

Michael A. Ledeen
Resident Scholar

Susan Lee
DeWitt Wallace Fellow in
Communications in a Free Society

Robert A. Licht
Resident Scholar

Chong-Pin Lin
Associate Director, China Studies
Program

John H. Makin
Resident Scholar

Allan H. Meltzer
Visiting Scholar

Joshua Muravchik
Resident Scholar

Charles Murray
Bradley Fellow

Michael Novak
George F. Jewett Scholar;
Director, Social and
Political Studies

Norman J. Ornstein
Resident Scholar

Richard N. Perle
Resident Fellow

Thomas W. Robinson
Director, China Studies Program

William Schneider
Resident Fellow

Herbert Stein
Senior Fellow

Irwin M. Stelzer
Resident Fellow

Edward Styles
Director, Publications

W. Allen Wallis
Resident Scholar

Ben J. Wattenberg
Senior Fellow

Carolyn L. Weaver
Resident Scholar

A NOTE ON THE BOOK

This book was edited by Ann Petty
of the publications staff
of the AEI Press.
The index was prepared by Julia Petrakis.
The text was set in Palatino, a typeface designed by
the twentieth-century Swiss designer Hermann Zapf.

The AEI PRESS is the publisher for the American Enterprise Institute for
Public Policy Research, 1150 17th Street, N.W., Washington, D.C. 20036:
Christopher C. DeMuth, publisher; *Edward Styles*, director; *Dana Lane*,
assistant director; *Ann Petty*, editor; *Cheryl Weissman*, editor; *Susan Moran*,
editorial assistant (rights and permissions).